EXPLORING THE PURCELL WILDERNESS

Exploring the Purcell Wilderness

Anne Edwards, Patrick Morrow, and Arthur Twomey

Douglas & McIntyre

Vancouver

Douglas & McIntyre
1875 Welch Street
North Vancouver,
British Columbia

Canadian Cataloguing in Publication Data

Edwards, Anne.
  Exploring the Purcell Wilderness

  ISBN 0-88894-176-5 pa.
  p. 102

  1. Trails - British Columbia - Purcell
Range. 2. Hiking - British Columbia - Purcell
Range. 3. Purcell Range - Description and
travel - Guide-books. I. Morrow, Pat. II.
Twomey, Art. III. Title.
FC3845.P8E38   917.11′45   C78-002038-3
F1089.P8E38

Typesetting by The Typeworks
Photography by Pat Morrow and Art Twomey
Maps by Don Schacher
Cover design by Nancy Legue-Grout
Printed and bound in Canada by Hignell Printing Limited, Manitoba

South fork of Toby Creek

Contents

Preface

This book is based on the premise that wilderness experience is significant. The person who never penetrates the wilderness misses something of lasting value. The one who enters alone or shares the experience with a few companions will be immeasurably enriched.

Man, the animal whose identifying trait has been his ability to alter his environment to suit his fancy, when entering the wilderness must join the other animals in adjusting his way to that of his environment. He will go where his own muscles will carry him; will wet his body and his clothing crossing streams; will be slowed by rain or wind; will share his space with bear, cougar, wood tick and honey bee; will test, alone, slopes and footings. Few of the trappings of civilization will benefit him here.

A friend defines wilderness as a place where you could be eaten. As far as it goes, the definition is a good one. Part of the wilderness experience is the recognition that we can fall prey to the kinds of danger from which we elaborately protect ourselves in urban centres. But more than that is the sense of belonging with the creatures that may eat us. We can become part of a rhythm, a pattern. We read the trees and rocks; we observe animals without disturbing them, and they return the courtesy. We belong to the land, just as do the butterflies and the bears; the fact is not hidden under concrete or distorted by artificial light.

The Purcell mountains, largely untouched by man's organizing hand, contain the first wilderness conservancy to be established in British Columbia. The protection afforded by this designation makes the area signally valuable for those who truly wish to recreate. The settled trenches on either side of the range offer the amenities of active, modern communities; within a few days' hiking are mature forests, evidence of geological development over centuries, and a vast array of plant and animal species, some of which are so rare as to be endangered.

The invitation that goes with this book to visit the Purcells and to enjoy a wilderness experience carries the belief that the experience will promote in the visitor a nurturing response, a recognition of the ability of the wilderness to compensate for the deficiencies of urban living, and a desire to preserve and expand the qualities the wilderness offers. Our philosophy complements a statement of Goethe: "We must earn again for ourselves that which we have inherited."

Horsethief Creek Falls

Introduction

Canada's national parks lie, one next to the other, along the British Columbia-Alberta border and westward along the route of the Trans-Canada railway and highway. The Purcells sit within the angle that they form. Lacking detailed maps until at least the 1930s and overshadowed in fame by the ranges contained within the national parks, they have been the playground of a very few. Only some of the trails were made by the Indians, who generally preferred to go around the range when crossing from East to West Kootenay for fish or game. After the Wildhorse Gold Rush of 1864 and the consequent fanning out into the surrounding area of prospectors, mines were established and trails were worn by miners searching for more gold or carrying their ore to main transportation routes and government inspection offices. Outfitters, too, developed access routes throughout the range. At about the turn of the century, lumbering began as an industry, and forest companies built roads into river drainages to gather their harvest. Trappers have made a living in the Purcells, and guides have taken advantage of the special nature of the area. (There is more variety of big game in this small area than in any other in North America.) Although guides and trappers can be quite secretive about their routes, trails do exist, lacing the whole range.

Until 1974 only two small sections of the Purcells were protected by the government as recreation areas: tiny St. Mary Alpine Park, on the upper drainage of White Creek, high above Spade Lake, and the one-square mile Bugaboo provincial park. Logging companies had taken over from mining companies as the major users of the land, and logging operations were being pushed farther up the slopes as well as moving into all the river valleys. In response to a substantial citizens' movement, the British Columbia government declared 325,000 acres the Purcell Wilderness Conservancy. The conservancy includes the core of a 1.5-million-acre area and covers the sources of the rivers draining the central Purcells. At the same time, a recreational reserve was put on Fry and Carney creeks on the west slope of the Purcells. Fry Canyon, steep and untouched, is thus protected from the ravages of industry and remains one of the most beautiful and accessible retreats for wilderness seekers.

The conservancy designation precludes installation of the kind of tourist amenities common to parks. There are no designated campgrounds, picnic tables or outdoor privies in the Purcells. The recreationist must adjust his ways to the ways of the wilderness.

High camp, Southern Purcells

Wading glacier-fed Horsethief Creek

Soaking in Dewar Creek hot springs

Some of the most spectacular parts of the Purcells are deep within the range; this means that the long-range hiker can anticipate a far greater reward than the day hiker, though there are numerous valley-bottom trails suitable for a family or other group that chooses not to camp overnight. In some places, however, the hiker is condemned to walk for miles through the miserable debris of a clear cut logging operation. We urge you to avoid such disappointing marches by checking beforehand with government officials or other knowledgeable local people about the location of these operations.

A hiking guide of the early century suggests that hikers of the Dogtooth mountains (the northern part of the Purcells) must be "intrepid persons indifferent to difficulties." We do not suggest that all hikers in the Purcells need to be describable in these terms. Many parts of the range present difficulties; indeed, some areas require great endurance to penetrate, and some provide a keen challenge to the world's best mountaineers. But one need not climb a rock face in order to appreciate its beauty. The general hiker, conspicuously not "indifferent to difficulties," can easily enjoy the Purcells. He can penetrate the range in a relatively short time if he chooses and can see dense forests and alpine meadows, observe the eagle and the goat, enjoy the quietest pool or the whitest of falling waters. A genuine wilderness experience awaits him.

Social History

Since over the years only a few hardy individualists have inhabited the Purcell Range, to talk of its social history is to talk of the people who have lived on either side of the range in the Rocky Mountain and Purcell trenches.

The Rocky Mountain Trench was the home of the Kootenay (sometimes spelled Kootenai) Indians, about whose origins no agreement has been reached. Whatever their origins, their language and practices were highly distinct from those of other tribes, and they occasionally had to fend off attack from the warlike Plains Indians of the eastern prairies.

The Rockies were crossed via Howse Pass in 1800 by Lagasse and Leblanc, two white employees of the North West Company working for David Thompson. Thompson himself came in 1807 and wintered at Kootenae House on Lake Windermere. His trading activities were combined with his extensive exploration of the Columbia River. Thompson travelled nearly the whole of the Columbia's course, eager to follow it to its mouth and claim the territory through which it ran for the British Crown so that his trading company (the North West, and later the Hudson's Bay Company) could enjoy the terms of its charter. He reached the mouth in 1811, too late to be the first to discover it, for the American Robert Gray had done so, approaching the river from the Pacific Ocean in 1792.

Nonetheless Thompson's influence was great on the traffic in the Rocky Mountain Trench from Eastern Canada and the Prairies. When the Howse Pass route through the Rockies became impracticable because of Indian hostility, Thompson discovered the Athabasca route which kept trade lines open for the 50 years or so that fur trading continued to flourish.

Thompson measured the height of some of the mountains, naming everything west of the Rocky Mountain Trench "Nelson's Mountains," after the hero of the Battle of Trafalgar, which had recently taken place. He named Columbia Lake as the source of the Columbia River, and noted in his diary the phenomenon of the Kootenay and Columbia rivers flowing within a mile of each other in opposite directions up and down the Trench.

Other travellers included Father De Smet, who came as a missionary through the West and East Kootenays in the 1840s. On his first trip he baptized the wife and children of François Morigeau, probably the first white settler in the Kootenays. Morigeau, born near Québec, had settled on Columbia Lake in 1819. In 1846 Paul Kane made his artistic pilgrimage to record on canvas and paper the life of the west. He travelled through the Rocky Mountain Trench and via the Columbia River to its mouth.

The first major inrush of white men was triggered by George Findlay's discovery of $700 worth of pumpkin seed gold on the creek which now bears his name. Findlay was a man of Indian and white ancestry. On his way through the area in the fall of 1863 to partake of a bit of high life in Montana, he sold the gold to the Hudson's Bay factor at Tobacco Plains. The news spread.

By 15 March 1864 a party of men had come in from Hellgate, Montana. Finding Findlay Creek still blocked by ice, they camped at Bummers' Flats near Wasa Lake. A second group consisting of five men came just days later from Walla Walla, Washington. Three went to Findlay, but the other two along with some of the first party spent their time panning the Kootenay at the mouth of a creek now known as Wild Horse Creek. They found enough gold there to draw them on, and three or four miles up the creek they struck rich ground. They named the creek Stud Horse Creek after a fine black cayuse stud that they saw high on its banks. The name was later changed, some say to suit finer sensibilities.

There were some 3,000 miners that summer on the Wild Horse, about 100 on Findlay Creek and between 100 and 200 prospecting in other parts of the Kootenays. Fisherville sprang up on Wild Horse as the centre of activities, with a population which approximated 10,000 at its peak. The biggest season on Wild Horse was 1865, when there were up to 8,000 miners. As in other gold rushes, provisions were so scarce that prices went sky high: flour sold at $1.25 a pound and tobacco cost as much as $17 a pound. Sellers were known to soak tobacco overnight in the stream to make it weigh more. Portuguese Joe left the country with $50,000 made butchering for the miners.

It is impossible to know how much gold was taken out of Wild Horse Creek, but certainly it paid better than any California creek in the palmy days of the California gold rush. Estimates of $15 to $17 million are probably close for the two- to-three year span of the rush itself. Government records account for $9 million, but smuggling was rampant, as the government had placed a tax of 50¢ an ounce on all gold taken out of the country.

Gold seekers are fickle, and news of strikes in the Yukon drew many miners away. Other social and economic activity took most of the rest, so that in 1880 there were only 11 white settlers in the East Kootenay and but one in the West Kootenay: Dick Fry, who lived at what is now Bonners Ferry. Mineral discoveries would bring people back again, but on a less extravagant basis.

7

The Blue Bell mine at Riondel was discovered in 1882, the Silver King at Nelson in 1887, the Alice Mine at Creston in 1890, the Slocan Silver in 1891, the North Star at Kimberley before 1892, and the St. Eugene mine at Moyie in 1892. By that time, a number of things had happened. Baillie-Grohman had built locks, hoping to join the Kootenay River to Columbia Lake in order to divert the water and make arable the Kootenay flats at Creston, but the scheme failed. In Kaslo, Col. Robert Lowery had established the first of his newspapers, which were, over the next 30 years, to become the miners' Bible. The Canadian Pacific Railway had been completed through Donald and Golden to the north, riverboats were plying the waters on either side of the Purcells, and coal had been discovered at Fernie. During the early 1890s the southern route of the CPR line was built, along with a number of other spur lines up and down the valleys. Besides lonely prospectors, the population in 1900 included hired miners, loggers, farmers, provisioners and innkeepers, doctors, lawyers, and Indian chiefs.

Today settlement remains at the feet of the Purcells, even though many of the major riches have come from the high mountains. Mining, forestry, tourism, and agriculture are the area's economic mainstays. Guides and hunters pursue a wide variety of game animals, and trappers seek the fur-bearing species.

Conflicting pressures from all the users of the Purcells led in 1973 to a government-commissioned study of the range, the establishment of a 325,000-acre wildlife conservancy covering the headwaters of the St. Mary River, the imposition of a recreational reserve on Fry and Carney creeks, and a co-ordinated approach by government to the management of this range that 30 years earlier had not even been fully mapped.

Establishment of the conservancy, the first in British Columbia, makes available to outdoors people an experience so rare as to be greatly treasured by those with the stamina to reach the heart of this ancient mountain range. As well, the natural beauty and rich plant, animal, land and water resources of the area make it rewarding for those who penetrate a lesser distance. Among the local population are those who value the natural resource of the area as greatly as they do any financial opportunity it proffers.

(left to right) *Wall Tower; Block Tower; Leaning Tower (Hall Peak)*

Physical Features

Various ranges of mountains sprawl across British Columbia between the Rockies, which mark its easternmost boundary, and the Coast Range, which edges the western coast. The Purcell Range is the easternmost of these, facing the Rockies across the long Rocky Mountain Trench and snuggling into the curve of the Selkirks, of which it has sometimes been labelled a part.

The Purcell watershed feeds the interlocking Columbia-Kootenay river system, but its intimacy with the Kootenay is the greater, for the range extends south into the northern United States to the bend of the Kootenay, but extends north with the Columbia only a short way to its intersection with the Beaver River.

The Purcells' first tourists, J. A. Lees and W. J. Clutterbuck, were accurate for their day in their description (in *B.C. 1887: A Ramble in British Columbia*) of the physical course of the two major rivers, and far more amusing than most travel writers:

> Close to the intersection of lat. 50° and long. 116° is the Upper Columbia Lake, the head waters of the mighty river of that name, which flows out of the lake in a northerly direction. It will be seen that another river, the Kootenay, which rises in the Rockies north of this point, almost runs into the same lake, the strip of land which separates them being in fact little more than a mile in width. Having avoided that premature termination to his career, the Kootenay continues his southerly course across the border into Montana and Idaho. There, apparently not thinking so much of Republican institutions as those who have not tried them are apt to do, he takes a sudden turn northwards, and again becomes a British river shortly before flowing in placid grandeur into the great Kootenay Lake. In the meantime the Columbia, repenting of the precipitate behaviour which led her to turn her back on the Kootenay in the giddy days of her youth, has about lat. 52° made an equally sudden turn to the south, and arrived so close to the Kootenay that it is an easy matter for the latter to simply rush into the arms of his long-lost love; after which they no doubt live happily ever afterwards. The result of this coquettish separation and subsequent reunion is that the land on which the Selkirks stand would be an island but for the narrow isthmus close to the Columbia Lake already spoken of.

The mountain ranges enclosed by these two rivers are the Purcells and the Selkirks. The dividing line between them follows the Purcell Trench from where the Kootenay re-enters Canada, along the north-south axis of

Kootenay Lake and the Duncan River up to and along the Beaver River, past Golden to the Beaver's intersection with the Columbia.

The Purcell oblong is about 60 miles (90 km) wide and 225 miles (360 km) long. By far the more interesting part for hikers is the 175-mile Canadian section. South of the border, where the Kootenay is spelled "Kootenai," the Purcells have shrunk to foothills and the main recreational interest is fishing. Farther north, the land has been called "a most formidable tract where even the banks of the rivers are cloud-capped mountains."

The Purcells are many millions of years older than their neighbouring Rockies, having been the original line of demarcation along the Cordilleran syncline. Along their edge, the ocean alternately advanced and receded from the continent over geological ages. They were mountains 1,200 to 1,600 million years ago when blue-green algae had made way for bacteria and seaweeds, and their profile alternately rose and fell through the ascendancies of the invertebrates, amphibians and reptiles. Only 70 million years ago, as toothed birds and flying reptiles overshadowed the armoured and horned dinosaurs, and mammals came into their own, did pressure from the west fold and fault the Cordilleran syncline into the Rocky Mountain Range, and the Purcells were replaced by the Rockies as the eastern edge of the continental highlands.

The range's age shows in its rock forms: its mountains are composed mainly of sedimentary rocks, including argillites, sandstones and limestones which contain fossil stromatolites. Of great interest to the mountain climber are the numerous granitic intrusions emplaced among the ancient Purcell rocks only a few thousand years after the Rockies had been thrust up. They comprise such well-known formations as the Bugaboos, the Leaning Towers, and the St. Mary Batholith. In fact, the Purcells expose the oldest rock to be found on the North American continent, save in the Grand Canyon.

The Purcells are generally 1,000 to 2,000 feet (304 to 609 m) lower in elevation than the Rockies, but they have more high peaks than the Selkirks. There are more than 50 peaks of 10,000 to 11,000 feet (3408 to 3353 m) altitude, the highest being Mount Farnham at 11,342 feet (3457 m). Purcell peaks seem higher than those of the Rockies because of the greater vertical distance between the valleys and the peaks. Valleys in the Purcells are 500 to 1,200 feet (152 to 366 m) lower than those in the Rockies. The

Glacier-carved U-shaped valley, head of Campbell Creek

high relief is exemplified on the shores of Kootenay Lake, elevation 1,756 feet (535 m), where the Purcells rise abruptly to 7,000 and 8,000 feet (2123 and 2438 m).

A vertical profile of the range looking north would show a rough triangle with the Purcell Trench on the left (west), the Rocky Mountain Trench on the right (east) and, considerably towards the west, the watershed as the apex. This conformation in conjunction with the prevailing westerly winds gives the two sides their highly individual character.

On the western-facing slope, vegetation is dense, the slope is steep, and precipitation is high, ranging from 40 to 50 inches (101 cm to 126 cm) per year. On the east, the creeks are longer, the valleys wider and less steep and the vegetation slightly less dense, with precipitation along the semi-arid Rocky Mountain Trench averaging only 15 inches (37.5 cm) per year. The sub-alpine forest zone extends in the Purcells up to the 6,000 to 7,000 foot (1829 to 2134 m) level on both sides of the divide, with some 50 inches (127 cm) or more per year of precipitation. Above timber line, four areas on the western slope of the Purcells are classed as alpine zone, with even higher precipitation.

The moisture-laden winds from the Pacific have been robbed many times before they reach the Purcells, but they leave enough precipitation to perpetuate numerous neves and glaciers, the leftover shreds of the last continental Ice Age. Evidence of glaciation is everywhere; only a handful of peaks escaped ice erosion. Although trees mask the scars to nearly the 7,000-foot (2134 m) level, U-shaped valleys and many waterfalls testify to the carving action of the ice as it flowed southward during the last Ice Age.

Much readier access on the eastern slope has led to forest and mining development and a proliferation of roads. But the difficulty of access on the west has helped preserve virgin forest along Fry and Hamill creeks, tributaries to Kootenay Lake. Some trail building and clearing has been done in recent years on both sides of the divide, improving access for the average hiker.

It is still true that the Rocky Mountain Trench is the traffic artery, the Purcell Trench having been opened mainly for local access, but the tourist can reach trail heads on either side of the Purcells. In each case he will find a distinct flavor to the experience offered, one that comes from the relative isolation that the Purcells have enjoyed.

Flora

Forest or biotic zones within the Purcells vary from the dry to the wet and include a high proportion, for the small area covered, of the truly alpine landscape of B.C.

The dry interior zone covers the Rocky Mountain Trench which borders the Purcells and that part of the Purcell Trench from its southern limit about half way to Crawford Bay. Plains and rolling hills at an altitude of about 3,000 feet (914 m) characterize the landscape. Annual precipitation measures up to 15 inches (37.5 cm); 40 per cent of that is snow. Summers are dry and warm and winters are relatively mild, with temperatures usually between 0° and -20 °C but sometimes dropping to -35 °C for short periods.

In this area the yellow or ponderosa pine is the dominant tree species, with Douglas fir and western larch intermingled. Black cottonwood takes over river bottoms and grows beside lakes, along with willow and red osier or shrub dogwood. Also commonly found are aspen, black birch, western choke cherry, dwarf and Rocky Mountain juniper, and mountain alder. Ground cover includes antelope bush, soopolallie, Oregon grape, saskatoon berry, raspberry, clematis and wild rose. Some of the flowers are: brown-eyed Susan and blue-eyed Mary, bitterroot, primrose, fleabane, Indian paintbrush, lupine, mariposa lily, mountain lady slipper, phacelia, sagewort, sheep sorrel, spring sunflower, woolly thistle and yarrow.

The interior wet belt, sometimes called the Columbia Forest Zone, occupies the valley bottoms along Kootenay Lake. There is a small bit of it on the eastern side of the Purcells on the St. Mary River about 25 miles upstream from the Kootenay River confluence. The transition between this zone and that of the dry interior is abrupt. Western or red cedar is the climax species in this fairly cold zone which reaches, on the western slope, up to about 3,500 feet (1050 m) altitude. Precipitation is quite high, averaging between 40 and 50 inches (60 and 75 cm) per year. There is a considerable intrusion of paper birch, western hemlock and western white pine, and you may also find Douglas fir, western hemlock, lodgepole pine, Engelmann spruce, western yew, dwarf and Rocky Mountain juniper, aspen, black cottonwood, black birch, white birch, bitter cherry, mountain alder and Douglas maple. Undergrowth is dense and may include: devil's club, elder, false azalea, gooseberry, honeysuckle, huckleberry, goat's beard, Indian hemp, kinnikinnick, mountain ash, raspberry, red-osier dogwood, rhododendron, squashberry, teaberry, thimbleberry, twinflower and

15

western anemone

calypso orchid

beargrass

Columbian lily

waxberry. Flowers include: alumroot, bleeding heart, bunchberry, chocolate lily, columbine, cow parsnip, fairy bells, false asphoden, false lady's slipper, false Solomon's seal, Indian paintbrush, large purple aster, lupine, moccasin flower, mountain lily, rattlesnake plantain, sarsaparilla, skunk cabbage, star-flowered Solomon's seal, snow lily and wild tiger lily.

The sub-alpine forest zone occupies the next highest level, ending at tree line: about 5,500 feet (1676 m) on the western slope and about 6,000 feet (1829 m) on the drier eastern side. This is a fairly humid coniferous forest belt—its annual precipitation is more than 50 inches (75 cm)—with a surface that is dissected by projecting peaks and trough-like valleys terminating in cirques (basins) which are often modified by talus slides. Alpine fir and Engelmann spruce are the dominant species; Lyall's larch and white-barked pine become more numerous near timber line. Douglas fir is still there, and white spruce, lodgepole pine, dwarf juniper, aspen, mountain and Sitka alder. Shrubbery includes white rhododendron or mountain misery, false azalea, several species of huckleberry, various heathers, kinnikinnick, Labrador tea, soopolallie, teaberry, thimbleberry and twinflower.

The alpine area is that above timber line. Without the protection of trees, the peaks experience severe weather conditions. The winters are long, the summers short. In the Purcells the prolongation of winter at the peaks because of the lingering snow is exaggerated by the many icefields. Some shrubs cling to the rocks; in damp places, dwarf willow springs up as predictably as ordinary willow around a slough. Moss and false heather can also be found, with American laurel and a thick turf of sedge around alpine tarns. There is alpine blueberry and black mountain huckleberry, as well as blackberry elder, Labrador tea and trailing azalea. Here the alpine flowers come into their own; we do not have the room to list even half. There is broad-leaf arnica, columbine, white and yellow dryas, cushion eriogonum, false forget-me-not, gentian, grass of Parnassus, Indian hellebore, Indian paintbrush, lady's tresses, moss campion, mountain daisy, mountain valerian, western anemone, wood betony, lupine, elephant head and white rein orchis.

Purcell ferns include the woodsia, parsley fern or rock brake, licorice fern, lady fern, bracken and some maidenhair.

There are many edible plants in the Purcells, but we strongly urge you to acquire basic knowledge of natural food before sampling any, as there are dangers involved in eating unknown substances. A book list on page 103 suggests several books to consult on edible wild plants.

Fauna

The Purcell Range catches enough moisture from the prevailing westerly winds to support rich forest and undergrowth and, consequently, abundant fauna. Big game was particularly plentiful during the 1940s and 1950s, in consequence of the many forest fires that swept through in the '20s and '30s as hordes of loggers and miners penetrated the previous wilderness. The fires opened grazing meadows where game found plenty of food next to the cover of the forest trees.

In the range can be found caribou, elk, moose, goat, white-tailed and mule deer, cougar, wolf, and black and grizzly bear. The habitat is too wet for mountain sheep, which are found in the Rocky Mountain Trench and farther east in the Rockies where the plains are semi-arid.

There are at least three distinct herds of mountain caribou in the Purcells. One roams the Sanca-Gray Creek area, another the Moyie Watershed, and a third the southern portion of the Wilderness Conservancy in the drainages of St. Mary River, Fry Creek and Carney Creek. They feed on tree lichens that survive only in mature forests. The caribou, feared to be a disappearing species, is not the only species in the Purcells sensitive to the advances of civilization. The mountain goat, grizzly bear, wolf, and wolverine are others which require special attention.

Rocky Mountain elk are not native to the Purcells but now exist there in fairly large numbers. A herd was transplanted to the Lardeau country in 1948 by the Fish and Wildlife Branch, and it has multiplied and spread both east and west.

Among these animals, some invite special note. The fisher is an extremely rare animal; it has been described as looking "half-way between" a wolverine and a weasel or marten. The provincial Wildlife Branch requests that any sightings be reported at their offices in Cranbrook or Nelson, or through a game warden. The red foxes are not true natives but are relatives of some which escaped from fur farms at Invermere around the turn of the century. Wolves are sighted mainly in the northern extent of the range, though there have been indeterminate reports of wolves in the southern Purcells. The hoary marmot is more often heard than seen. Elizabeth Parker, in her book *The Selkirk Mountains,* says of the marmot's alarm-sounding whistle: "It sounds exactly like that shrill far-penetrating whistle contrived with various aids by the human boy." The navigator shrew is a diving animal that lives in water. And as for the

marten

marmot

elk in early summer

woodchuck, though it is listed in every book on the area, no one remembers its ever having been seen.

The list of animals a hiker or skier may see in the Purcells include:

mountain goat	wolf
mountain caribou	coyote
B.C. moose	porcupine
white-tailed deer	mouse
mule deer	vole
Rocky Mountain elk	pack rat
Canadian lynx	muskrat
bobcat (at lower elevations)	beaver
cougar (associated with mule deer herds)	hoary marmot
	lemming
otter	flying squirrel (rare)
skunk	Douglas squirrel (red squirrel)
striped skunk	chipmunk
yellow badger	Columbian ground squirrel
wolverine	mantled ground squirrel
mink	woodchuck
weasel	varying hare (changes colours by season)
fisher	
marten	Rocky Mountain pika
grizzly bear	bat (little brown)
black bear	navigator shrew
red fox	dusky shrew

The most troublesome animal to campers and hikers is likely to be the porcupine. This spiny creature will eat almost anything, and campers are urged to protect not only their food but also their tires. Porcupines have been particularly numerous in the White Creek (east fork of the St. Mary River) area, and anyone who plans to leave a vehicle there while he ventures forth on foot is advised to carry some chicken wire. Surround the vehicle with the wire, weighted down at the bottom with stones and affixed as well as possible at the top. Porcupines have an especial fondness for rubber; they have been known to chew tires to shreds and to climb under the hood of a car or truck to sample the hoses and other connections.

The Purcell is bear country. There are those who say that part of the wilderness experience is to lie awake nights, imagining that a bear (black or grizzly, as the script-writer prefers) is stalking you and/or your food, is about to attack you in your bedroll, or is intent on chewing your leg as you scramble up a spindly tree. However, bears prefer to avoid you. In order to attract them, you would have to leave your food open and unprotected. Unprotected food could prompt a bear to wreck your camp in search for more, but if he is not initially attracted, he is likely to steer clear of you.

The best weapon in avoiding a confrontation with a bear is distance. This can usually be maintained by using your eyes and the bear's ears. In other words, keep an eye out while you are hiking. Look beyond the trail; occasionally scan the countryside with binoculars, if you carry them. Watch for both bear and carrion, for there may well be a bear near a dead animal. Other carrion-eaters—magpies and ravens, for example—could serve as advance warning.

To use the bear's ears, you must make some noise as you travel. Put a bear bell on your packsack, or pound a can with a stick. Some people make a racket with a rock in an empty can. Whistle, as long as you do not imitate the whistle of the marmot. The human voice, many think, carries farthest. Talk loudly, sing, or practise your yodelling. It is far better for a bear to scent or hear you before seeing you. Before you start your hike, enquire of local officials or other hikers about recent sightings of bears.

There are several rules for campers in bear country. Camp away from trails; bears use trails, just as humans do. Camp under trees, noting which ones can be most easily climbed. Cook cleanly and stow your garbage. Highly odorous foods, such as ham, bacon and fish, must be handled very carefully or avoided. Cook away from your sleeping area, and then stow both food and waste in airtight containers, such as sealed plastic bags. Food can be slung from a pole suspended at least 12 feet off the ground, or it can be cached in an inconspicuous location on the ground, though the latter option is less safe. Cooking utensils should also be kept away from your bed area and out of reach of bears, if possible. Make sure that there is no bear around before you approach your cache of food or utensils to retrieve them.

Waste can be burned, as long as it is completely burned, but ashes should be sifted to check for food traces before leaving a camp to which you will return. If a bear visits your camp, move it; *there is no maybe about this*. At night keep a flashlight handy, and also a noisemaker, if you have one.

Andy Russell's *Grizzly Country* makes excellent reading for those who would be prepared to travel in grizzly country; another good book is *No Room for Bears* by Frank Dufresne. Outdoor magazines often run excellent articles on the subject, and any experienced wildlife biologist can help you realize a feeling of competence in bear country.

Birds

More than 20 varieties of birds are resident in the Purcells, and transients on their way through as well as seasonal visitors fill out the magnificent roster. The whole area is part of the Mississippi flyway, the main inland migratory route for North American birds on their way from the north to Central or South America in the fall and back in the spring. Some of these migratory birds nest in the Purcell area: for example, there are large concentrations of geese in the Columbia River flats between Invermere and Golden, and swans in the Creston Wildlife Management Area on the Kootenay marshes near Creston.

Resident birds include:

golden eagle	Clark nutcracker
blue grouse	black-capped chickadee
Franklin grouse	mountain chickadee
ruffed grouse	white-breasted nuthatch
pileated woodpecker	red-breasted nuthatch
hairy woodpecker	pygmy nuthatch (scarce)
American three-toed woodpecker	brown creeper (scarce)
Canada jay	dipper
black-billed magpie	winter wren
raven	golden-crowned kinglet
English sparrow	red crossbill

The following birds commonly visit in the summer and may winter over if the weather is good: goshawk; belted kingfisher; Wilson snipe; red-shafted flicker; Townsend solitair; horned grebe; American merganser.

Bird names being so fascinating in themselves, it is tempting to tell of the olive-sided flycatcher and other scarce summer visitant species, but the numbers of birds that have been sighted are altogether too great to be listed in this type of book. We refer those with a special interest in bird-life to the book list on page 103.

Walter B. Johnstone in a book entitled *An Annotated List of the Birds of the East Kootenay, B. C.* (unfortunately now out of print) related details of the sighting of a dipper, about which he concluded that it must be highly immune to cold temperatures. The sighting occurred on a winter day when the air temperature was $-25\,°F$, and the dipper was diving into a pool, sometimes through ice crystals, and bringing back leaves from the bottom of the pond. The bird would inspect the leaves for insect life, on which he was making his meal, and his stamina was attested to by the collection of 27 such leaves on the ice beside him.

Here are some of the more common birds that might be sighted in the Purcells:

common loon	Hammond flycatcher
American bittern	violet-green swallow
Canada goose	tree swallow
snow goose	rough-winged swallow
mallard	barn swallow
pintail	American crow
baldpate	American robin
Turkey vulture	Swainson thrush
Cooper hawk	mountain bluebird
marsh hawk	ruby-crowned kinglet
sparrow hawk	Bohemian waxwing
duck hawk	cedar waxwing
osprey	red-eyed vireo
American coot	yellow warbler
killdeer plover	Audubon warbler
spotted sandpiper	yellow-throat
pectoral sandpiper	American redstart
herring gull	western meadowlark
ring-billed gull	Brewer blackbird
black tern	evening grosbeak
mourning dove	Cassin purple finch
horned owl	rosy finch
pygmy owl	savannah sparrow
nighthawk	vesper sparrow
rufous hummingbird	Oregon junco
Lewis woodpecker	chipping sparrow
yellow-bellied sapsucker	song sparrow
eastern kingbird	

Fish

The sportsman who is primarily interested in fishing will stay at the base of the Purcells, but the hiker-camper who ventures into the heights will usually be able to hook himself a good breakfast.

Perhaps the most sought-after game fish are the rainbow trout, Yellowstone cutthroat, Dolly Varden and kokanee, but there are also Rocky Mountain whitefish, eastern brook trout, ling and sturgeon to be caught.

The rainbow trout, here often called Kamloops trout, makes up the main part of the headwater populations of the creeks in the Purcells, but they are also sought at lower levels where they are much larger, the largest being found in the north arm of the lake. Perhaps the best place to fish rainbow in a stream is above the waterfall on the Fry River.

The Yellowstone cutthroat trout is indigenous to the Kootenays but to nowhere else in B.C. It repopulated in the Kootenays from the Mississippi river system after the last glacial age and is found in many of the streams. Dolly Varden is also indigenous to the area. Often called a bull trout, it is actually a char. The largest dollies are to be found in Kootenay Lake.

Fisherman at Baker Creek

Kokanee are landlocked salmon believed to have penetrated far into the interior to spawn at some time in past ages and to have been trapped. They are the fish of greatest abundance in Kootenay Lake, but in the East Kootenay they are found only in Moyie and Grave lakes. They spawn in the tributary streams, and thus are sometimes found outside of the lakes.

The watershed of the upper Columbia formerly supported spring salmon spawning, but the building of Grand Coulee Dam on the Columbia in the United States during the mid-1930s resulted in the total loss of these magnificent fish to the Purcells.

Eastern brook trout, commonly called speckled trout, were transplanted into the Moyie system early in this century and have become happy natives. They have now spread beyond the Moyie system, particularly since the advent of the Kootenay Fish Hatchery, which plants brook trout, rainbow and some cutthroat in more than 15 lakes at lower levels in the East Kootenay.

Rocky Mountain whitefish, often incorrectly referred to as grayling, are also indigenous to the Kootenays.

Because the waters of Columbia Lake and Windermere Lake are too warm, neither has a good salmonid fishery, but they do support good winter ling cod fishing. Ling of three to eight pounds can be caught in winter and spring in Windermere and Columbia lakes, the Kootenay River, and Kootenay and St. Mary lakes. Dutch and Bugaboo creeks and the Spillamacheen River have been stocked with ling, but at the time of writing the fish were still protected.

Huge sturgeon can also be caught in Kootenay Lake. Although most fishermen do not consider them good sport, they are an excellent eating fish.

Moyie Lake is the only body of water that contains every species of fish named, though not in large quantity. The Fish and Wildlife Branch planted the lake with Mycis shrimp in 1969 and 1970; the shrimp have taken hold, and an increased fish population is expected to follow.

Insects

By far the most rapacious, infuriating insect any hiker will find in the Purcells is the mosquito. It is persistent, irritating, blood-hungry, and whiningly noisy. Although it shuns the high points, where the breezes sweep it away, it holes up in the low spots near water where the camper invariably finds himself at one point during his trip. The mosquito is attracted by warmth and humidity, two elements offered innocently by the human species. The offending female mosquito needs the stimulus of carbon dioxide, given off by humans and other warm-blooded animals, before she starts a search for her prey: once she scents it, she is on a survival hunt for a blood meal in order to produce eggs. She needs only 30 seconds to suck her fill, leaving in trade an anticoagulant—the itching factor.

The mosquito has affected the whole history of the Purcell area, and not only by appearing in most of the written records (a Cranbrook portrait sketch book describes residents of the city as being "optimistic as mosquitoes"). The Kootenay Indians knew a spot just south of Cranbrook on Cranbrook Mountain, where they would gather in midsummer when the mosquitoes were at their worst at lower elevations. They would camp at the spot for weeks at a time, and it has seriously been suggested that their enforced idleness during these campouts was the inspiration for the petroglyphs which have been discovered on the mountain.

Indeed, the mosquito provided the inspiration for a number of the more interesting passages of the Lees and Clutterbuck travel book to which we have alluded. "There is no misery on earth equal to a really bad attack of these demons," they wrote.

In addition to mosquitoes, there are also horseflies and deerflies, wasps, ticks, cockroaches and some black widow spiders.

Ticks can be dangerous in the spring and early summer, and hikers are warned to check their persons and their clothing several times a day. The Rocky Mountain wood tick is the most dangerous, as it can transmit spotted fever, but the little brown tick is also dangerous. When removing a tick from your skin, in which it will have buried its head, do not try to pull it out. The body often breaks off, leaving the head behind to encourage infection. Rather, dab the tick with ammonia, turpentine, or gasoline; or hold a lighted cigarette near it, and it will back out of its burrow. Ticks are highly resistant to crushing, but may be destroyed by burning.

Winter Use

It is not hard to convince the outdoor enthusiast of the potential for winter recreation in the Purcells. One can almost always count on adequate snow cover to provide generally good skiing and snowshoeing conditions. The combination of relatively high valley elevation, moderate winter temperatures, and low winds provides a durable snow base. Pockets of skiable powder can be found in protected basins until late spring; indeed, given the right conditions, it is possible to ski the Purcells year round. Glacier skiing, particula.'y in the Bugaboos, is enticing to many.

Winter use of the Purcells has an honorable history. During the 1890s, prospector Fred M. Wells explored several passes from West to East Kootenay. He and a partner would trek through the Purcells on snowshoes, drawing toboggans. Wells preferred the Toby-Hamill Creek route, and the pass was originally named for him.

Early in this century Austrian-born guide Conrad Kain snowshoed from his home in Wilmer to make a solo ascent of Jumbo Peak, the Purcell's second highest mountain. In the 1960s ski guide Hans Gmoser pioneered a number of ski routes in the area, one of them being the Toby Creek to the Bugaboos. His party used traditional touring equipment: downhill skiis, boots, and climbing skins. In 1974 the Vallantine party made a traverse of the range from Argenta to Invermere. The seven-day trek covered 50 miles, including a final 26-mile slog along an unplowed road.

The trick for the interested skier and showshoer is reaching the powder. Those who have explored the area in winter often call the process "helicopter skiing sans helicopter." It involves making your way into the mountains on one of the few plowed logging roads and transporting enough gear to keep warm while you climb out of the trees and into powder-deep cirques. Because winter logging activities (and hence cleared roads) vary from year to year, it is necessary to check with local logging companies before planning your excursion (see trail section, p. 39).

In addition to day trips in the valley bottoms, there are a number of more adventurous trips which involve climbing into a basin, camping overnight, and skiing back down. There are also a few developed cross-country trails near Golden and Kimberley.

In the St. Mary area, skiing to the headwaters of Alki Creek and back—a day trip—provides good powder skiing. The gently graded road to the Paradise Mine site above Toby Creek offers another day or overnight trip. It is possible to climb to Boulder Camp in the Bugaboos and do a loop trip back to Gmoser's lodge via Cobalt Lake. Chalice Creek and Bugaboo Pass also make interesting day trips. Quartz Lake is a long day's ski from the Trans-Canada Highway near Golden, as is Gray Creek Pass from the Kootenay Lake side of the range.

A word of caution must be sounded. This is avalanche country, and the danger should not be underestimated. In early winter, powder avalanches can be easily triggered; in late winter, slab avalanches can be set off in exposed areas; and in spring, huge gully washers bring down tons of wet snow. Each member of a ski party should carry avalanche beepers and be checked out on the procedures to follow if caught in a snow slide. Needless to say, one should never ski or snowshoe alone. It is also important to be acquainted with the area's weather patterns, for winter travel in the Purcells is a serious business. Forewarned and properly equipped skiers and snowshoers will find the experience exhilarating.

High-country nordic skiing

Place Names

Interest in place names in the Purcells starts with the naming of the range itself. Some writers of long ago called the Purcells a westerly range of the Rockies—but then, they also referred to British Columbia as "New Caledonia."

When David Thompson produced his extensive map of 1813-14 covering 20 years of surveys and discoveries, he called all the mountains between the Columbia bend and the Kootenay bend Nelson's Mountains. When the North West Company and the Hudson's Bay Company amalgamated, the name was changed to Selkirk Mountains in honour of the Earl of Selkirk, the famous member of the HBC and founder of the Selkirk Colony on the Red River in Manitoba.

The Purcells were first designated as a range on the map prepared in 1859 by the Palliser Expedition which had been sent from England to investigate possible routes for railways across British North America. They were named for Goodwin Purcell, "The O'Leary," who had been a member of the committee to select officers for the expedition. Purcell, a medical doctor and noted teacher (he held the Chair of Therapeutics and Medical Jurisprudence in Queen's University, Cork) was also—from 1817 to 1876—the last chieftain of the line of O'Leary.

Despite the Palliser map, the two ranges of mountains continued to be called by many writers and mapmakers the Selkirks; consequently, much that you may read about the Purcells in the early days may be included with information about the Selkirks. The misnomer continued until this century when more extensive exploration finally established the separateness of the two ranges.

The Kootenay and Columbia rivers were also dealt a number of names in their time. Thompson called the Kootenay McGillivray's River after Duncan and William McGillivray, his superiors in the North West Company. He named the Columbia the Kootenae from the present Columbia Lake to its junction with Canoe River.

The mouth of the Columbia, however, had been discovered in 1775 by Heceta and named Rio de San Rogue. In 1792 it was rediscovered by an American, Robert Gray, who named it Columbia after his vessel. When Thompson discovered that the river he had named Kootenae was the same as Gray's Columbia, he gave the name Kootenay to the McGillivray River.

Columbia and Windermere lakes were originally called the Columbia lakes. There are a number of stories about the naming of Windermere Lake,

(top) *The Shining Range*; (bottom) *Mount Lees and Mount Clutterbuck*

the most likely one being that in 1883 G. M. Sproat named it after a lake named Windermere in his home area, the English lake country.

A white man's legend in Fred Smith's *Tales of the Kootenays* tells of the days when dinosaurs roamed this country and the people were also huge of stature. They roamed the plains, "lived and loved, ate and fought and died, just as do their pigmy successors of the present day." They used their magic to throw up great mounds, in long tiers, to hold back the main waters. Two of these people were Winder, he of the wind, and Mere, she of the sea. Beautiful and able, the two loved and mated. Their first child, a son, died, and griefstricken Mere soon followed him to the land of the Sinking Sun, where the gods buried them both.

Winder pined for his loved ones; lonely and forlorn, he yearly visited their graves. One year he did not return. The gods searched for him and found him prone, as if in a deep sleep, in the grass beside the valley graves of his wife and child. Rather than wake him to his grief again, they waved their wands over him, repeating the mystic words that made his body dissolve into the earth. "Sleep on, oh loved one; sleep on, but never cease to weep. Let your warm tears mingle with the waters that flow to the sea. Sleep on," said the gods.

Thus it is that Columbia Lake, warmed by Winder's tears of love and grief, never freezes; nor does the river for miles to the north, even in the coldest winters. This legend, of course includes little Mud Lake, located between Windermere and Columbia Lakes.

Kootenay River and Kootenay Lake, into which it empties, were named for the Kootenay Indians resident in the area. They were called The Lake People or Co-Tinneh, the compound word meaning "Water" and "People."

The following partial list of names has been included because they convey some touch of warmth, wit or human interest.

Birthday Peak—This peak was first ascended on Conrad Kain's thirty-first birthday by himself and Mr. and Mrs. A. H. MacCarthy, who, like Kain, had taken up residence in the Invermere area. The three of them made the first ascents of 15 Purcell peaks of more than 10,000 feet (3048 m).

Bugaboos—Bugaboo was the name given to a mining claim on a pass between Howser Peak and the Quintets, but it has come to be associated with the striking rock spires of the area. Finger after finger of granite clusters—called nunataks—seem to pierce the sky. They have been a challenge to those who would take their minerals or would climb them, and a visual treat to those who would simply enjoy them.

33

Commander Group—Mount Commander by its imposing looks alone deserves the name. Within the group are The Lieutenants, The Sargent (the source for this spelling is unknown) and The Guardsmen.

Cony Peak—Named in 1947 by Arnold Wexler, who described his experience on reaching the peak before any other known human: "We were not the first to reach the top, for the indignant beep of an unabashed and irreverent cony kept informing us in no uncertain terms that he had a prior claim to the mountain, and we were meddlesome intruders." (*Alpine Journal, Eugene F. Boss*)

Dogtooth Group—The mountains at the northern tip of the Purcells; not too high, similar to dog's teeth in shape, named by a person of some imaginative visual perception.

Duchess Peak—Named for the best-loved steamboat that plied the Columbia and Kootenay rivers before the advent of rail in the Rocky Mountain Trench. Other boats were honoured in the following names: Mount Hyak, Mount Gwendolin, North Star Peak, Nowitka Mountain, Midge Peak. The *Midge* was the boat imported from the U.S. by William Baillie-Grohman, who escaped paying a large duty on it because he said it was a farm implement likely to be used to haul a plow on the Creston flats.

Dutch Creek—People of Dutch origin used to fish where the creek flows into Columbia Lake.

Fry River—Dick Fry kept a ranch near Bonners Ferry. At one time, in the 1880s, he was the only white settler in the West Kootenay.

Horseman Spire—The party who first ascended this peak in 1953 had each, in reaching the peak, to straddle a knife-edged ridge, cowboy style, and thus wriggle across with nothing but 500 feet of air for each stirrup.

Horsethief Creek—An American and a Swede rustled some ponies from a whiskey peddler in 1885. The rustlers were pursued, captured, taken to Fort Steele, and, after trial, executed. Horsethief Creek is where they were captured.

Jumbo Mountain—Named when it was believed to be the highest peak in the Purcells. Actually it is the second-highest, the highest being Mount Farnham.

MacBeth Group—Includes MacBeth Mountain, Banquo Mountain, MacDuff Mountain and Fleance Mountain. It is said that they were so named because of their close proximity to Duncan Lake. (Shakespearean scholars need not be reminded that Duncan was the first victim of MacBeth's murderous hand, and the other three names are those of characters in the

34

play.) Duncan Lake and River, however, are said to have been named for an early prospector. Even though they appear on David Thompson's early map, they were *not* named for the Duncan McGillivray who was prominent in the North West Company.

Mount Conrad—The highest peak of the group named the Conrad group (formerly the Robbie Burns group) and on whose sides rest the Conrad Icefield. Conrad Kain was the best-known Austrian guide in the Purcells as well as a climber and guide of world-wide reputation. He was not only admired for his nearly superhuman feats but also held in great affection for his charm and his enthusiasm for telling anecdotes and tall tales. Kain made the first ascent of Mt. Robson, the highest peak in the Rockies, and of many of the highest peaks in the Purcells, including the Bugaboo spires. He made the first winter ascent of Jumbo Mountain.

Mount Ethelbert—Named By Capt. George Armstrong, a famous river-boat captain of the East Kootenay, for a nun who died on his boat *Ptarmigan*. She was, if not the first white woman to ascend the river, certainly the first nun to do so (in 1886).

Mount Lees and Mount Clutterbuck—Thorington's tribute to these two tourists of 1887, and their incomparable travel book about the tour, was to name for them two of the mountains he first ascended.

Mount Morigeau—François Morigeau, the first white settler, was a Québec free trader who came to the Kootenay via Tête Jaune Cache in 1819 and brought a bride of the Swampy Cree Indians. When she became lonesome for the prairie and went back, he brought a second wife from the Red River Colony in Manitoba. Their son Baptiste was the oldest man in the Kootenays when he died in 1932; he was about 88 years old. (His birth date was not certain, nor was his birthplace, which he described as being "in the glade.") His obituary said he was born at the headwaters of the Elk or the Columbia, and he lived most of his adult life on Windermere Lake.

Mount Truce and Mount Cauldron—The two were first ascended (by J. Monroe Thorington) on the same stormy day. The former was bathed in light, prismatically tinted, and the sight of it was taken as a good omen. The latter was surrounded by cloud masses which boiled and swirled over the peak, suggesting the convex currents of a witch's brew.

Radiant Peak—This peak was named at sunset, when it is indeed radiant.

Redtop Mountain—Originally Earl Grey Mountain, but caught up in the name-switching. Named for its reddish hue.

Approaching Bugaboo Spire from Boulder Camp

Saffron Peak—The hydrographic apex of the Purcells, it marks the division of drainage to the Columbia River, the Kootenay River, and Kootenay Lake. A yellow deposit appears in the water that flows from its glacier.

St. Mary River and Lake—The Blessed Virgin was patron saint of the Order of Mary Immaculate, to which belonged Father Foquet, who founded the St. Eugene Mission on the St. Mary River in 1874.

Shining Range—Includes Redtop, Blockhead and Earl Grey mountains. When icy and wet, the peaks make a magnificent display.

Skookumchuck Mountain—And a river, too. Skookum means "strong" in Chinook; Chuck means "water." It is not clear why the Chinook jargon was used.

Spillimacheen—A distortion of the Indian word Spil-a-mi-shine, which means "flat mouth."

Starbird Glacier—Named not for a bird, nor for an imaginative beauty caught in words, but for Thomas Starbird, a native of Massachusetts, who was one of the first mining men interested in the area. He financed the development of the Paradise Mine and established the Mountain Valley Ranch on Horsethief Creek, often used by paying guests. He explored the area around the Lake of the Hanging Glaciers (which he originally named Lake Maye for his wife); one of the glaciers draining into the lake is named for him, too.

Toby Group—Includes Toby Mountain and Toby Creek, named after a Spokane doctor who was also a prospector and was attracted to the Wild Horse gold rush. The group also includes Katherine, Christine and Griswold mountains. The latter was named by J. Monroe Thorington, an interested climber who did three stints in the Purcells with Conrad Kain, climbing and mapping, and who wrote one of the best books about the range. Thorington, Kain and two others traversed the three peaks in one day, and Thorington gave them the three parts of his wife's maiden name. Thorington also has a peak named after him.

Wells Peak—Fred M. Wells deserves to have a mountain named after him because his name was replaced for the pass over the Purcells between the headwaters of Toby and Hamill creeks. Wells was a prospector who travelled the pass summer and winter and who eventually, after 10 years of searching, found gold. The pass that used to bear his name was renamed Earl Grey Pass after the then Governor-General; he, his wife, and a party camped near the pass in 1909 and walked over from west to east, emerging at Invermere.

PURCELL MOUNTAIN RANGE

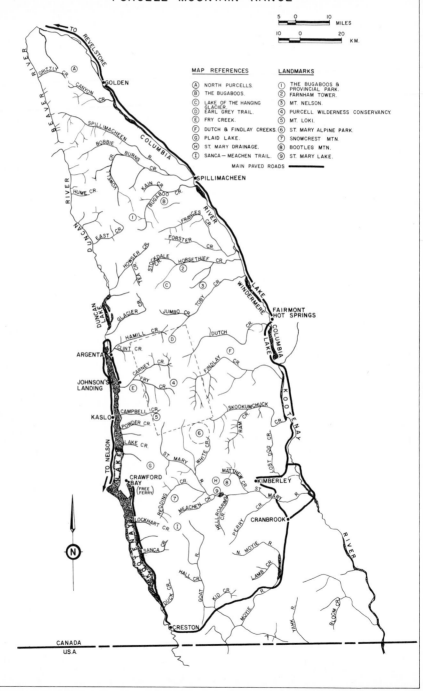

Trail Descriptions

Unless otherwise noted in the original description, most of the listed roads are primary logging or fire access roads, maintained by the British Columbia Forestry Service (BCFS). In some cases, after logging has taken its toll in certain valleys, the roads are kept up and used for fire access. But many roads are left to revert to nature, and were it not for enterprising sportsmen doing patch-up jobs and clearing out windfalls, many routes would be less accessible.

Since access roads are usually heavily used by logging trucks—seven days a week in summer—it would be wise to check with the nearest logging company about the best time to travel. Usually early morning is preferable, as that is when the trucks are coming from behind you rather than from in front. Companies to call are: (West Kootenay) West Kootenay Forest Products in Nelson; (East Kootenay) Crestbrook Forest Industries in Cranbrook, Canal Flats, or Parsons; Evans Forest Products in Golden; Revelstoke Logging in Radium.

Up-to-date information on roads and trails can also be obtained from BCFS ranger stations which are located in Cranbrook, Canal Flats, Invermere, Spillimacheen, Golden, Revelstoke, Lardeau, and Kaslo. Fish and Wildlife Branch offices in Nelson and Cranbrook should also be able to supply information.

Whereas there are a fair number of passable trails in the Purcells, most were built and heavily used prior to the 1930s. Unless someone has taken the initiative to reopen them—as in the case of the Earl Grey Trail—only remnants remain, the alder and buckbrush being quick to reclaim their territory. Old mining trails built above timber line will likely remain intact for hundreds of years, but the sections leading up to them through the forested valleys become overgrown nearly as fast as they are constructed. To accommodate the present interest in hiking, the BCFS is employing crews to open up the first few miles of trails along some creek drainages. After leaving newly opened trails, hikers will find topo maps and good map-reading skills handy.

The hiker will discover that his experience in the Purcells is far different from hiking the neighbouring national parks. On the whole, travel will be relatively slow, strenuous, and involved. In fact, a half-day hike could turn into a multi-day trip of some hardship should the hiker be ill-prepared for the unexpected. Underbrush could be much harder to penetrate than anticipated; weather could close in and dictate a halt; windfalls could necessitate a long detour.

Trails are subject to washouts and to obliteration by winter snow slides and fallen trees. Stream crossings as sophisticated as suspension bridges or as simple as single-log crossings are washed out regularly by spring floods. Logging roads, as they penetrate to the heart of the range, partially or entirely pre-empt some trails. For these reasons, hikers should contact regional forestry people for the latest trail information before making plans to visit the range.

Hiking times given in the legend of each trail description are estimates. Much depends on the interests and time schedules of the individual hiker. As in the Rockies, most trails ascend the valleys, so when planning round trips, you can assume that it will take less time to return to the road than it did to reach the high point. Because of the heavy residual snow pack, the best hiking months are July through October.

The maps included with the trail descriptions will give the hiker a general idea about his location but are not detailed enough to be used as specific guides. We advise the hiker to obtain the appropriate topographic map for his area of interest. Topo maps have a scale of 1:125,000, or 1 inch to 2 miles (5 km) and are available for purchase from the Map Production Division, B.C. Lands Service, Parliament Buildings, Victoria, B.C., as well as from local government agents. Some book stores carry topo maps. The Purcells are covered by maps labelled: Golden, Beaton, Invermere, Lardeau, Kaslo, Cranbrook, Elko, Creston. Where routefinding is complex, the more detailed maps with a scale of 1:50,000 are recommended.

As more people use the Purcell trails, hikers must take even more care to protect themselves and the environment. Already some bears are educated enough to investigate those camps which give off inviting food odours. Self-preservation demands careful attention to good housekeeping.

Preservation of the wilderness requires special measures also. Use a stove; it is safer and cleaner than a campfire. If you need to build a fire, do so on mineral soil or rock. Because fire pits are an eyesore along the trail, keep fires small and off the trail wherever possible.

Dig your latrine away from your camp and far from water supplies. Even for short stops while in transit, dig a hole, however shallow, as it is unsanitary to simply cover human waste with leaves or bracken.

Please respect alpine soil and foliage. Do not tear up plants or roll rocks down hills. The environment will not sustain the use of cedar boughs or bracken for bedding, so bring your own mats. Litter despoils. Remember that scrap paper discarded in creature burrows just comes back out when you are gone.

A word of caution: bridges that have not been washed out may have been weakened from snowload or from being hit during high water. Always cross carefully, one person at a time.

In the following descriptions, the letter after the trail title refers to a corresponding map. Some maps incorporate several trails; some trails are not shown except on the general map.

The legend at the beginning of each trail description gives relevant elevations and a topographical map reference. Because all described areas require a usually lengthy vehicular approach to the trailhead, the estimated time needed to reach one's destination and return have been given in day units rather than in hiking hours.

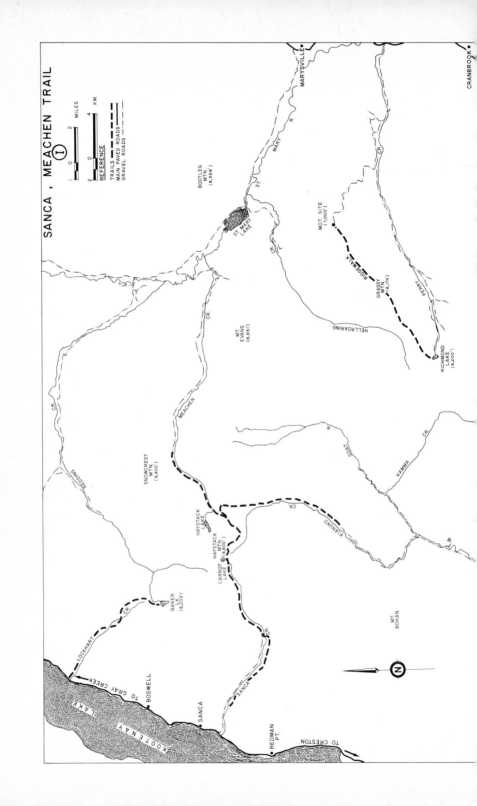

Sanca Creek to Meachen Creek (I)
(a lateral traverse of the range)

Allow 3 days for traverse
Kootenay Lake 2,000 feet (609 m)
Trail head 5,000 feet (1524 m)
Haystack Lake 6,200 feet (1890 m)
Height of land 7,000 feet (2134 m)
Kaslo-Cranbrook Topo

According to Wally Johnson, a trapper living at Sirdar, Ole Harris was a horse packer on the Sanca Creek trail in 1900, when Wally was born. Sirdar was a four-hotel town then, used as a jumping-off point for prospectors coming down the Kootenay River from Bonners Ferry, Idaho, and heading into the mine workings around White Grouse Mountain in the Meachen Creek drainage. A trail from the St. Mary side (Meachen Creek) linked up with the Sanca trail at the height of land beneath Haystack Mountain.

Today, logging roads being extended up both drainages have superseded the lower parts of the trails. In the summer of 1976 a Forestry crew working out of Creston opened up two sections of the Sanca trail to hikers, and Forestry officials say plans are underway to clear out the remaining distance between the upper reaches of Sanca and Meachen.

Also on the agenda for enlarging the Sanca trail system are plans to build trails into two fishing lakes: Sherman Lake, a good-sized lake on the east side of Mt. Sherman; and Wooden Shoe Lake, south of Sanca Creek, at the head of Skelly Creek.

The first 6 miles (9 km) of the Sanca trail, following the creek bottom and paralleling the new road, have been cleared. One hundred yards (91.4 m) north of the Sanca Creek bridge on Highway 3A, the dirt Sanca road swings east. About 300 yards (274 m) from the highway, a sign posted at the roadside denotes the start of the trail. Six miles (9 km) later it emerges onto the road, which continues another couple of miles and crosses the creek. At this point, stay on the north side of the creek, crossing the logging slash, until you pick up the trail. This continues another 4 miles (6 km) to the height of land and Carrot Lake (so named because this was the main commodity left in the dwindling food supplies of an early party in this area) at the base of the south slopes of Haystack mountain.

Along this upper part of the trail, sections of the old cedar-slat corduroy trail still span the mud holes. Hiking time to Carrot Lake is approximately 1½ hours from road's end.

Another route used by fishermen to get into the lakes at the head of Meachen Creek, is via a logging road up Goat River and Kianuko Creek, 22 miles (35 km) from Kitchener on Highway 95. The last 10 miles (16 km) are suitable only for four-wheel-drive vehicles unless the road is in ideal condition late in summer. From the end of the road on Kianuko Creek an outfitter's trail leads along the north branch of the creek until, in approximately 5 miles (8 km) it reaches the height of land and picks up the Meachen Creek trail, which can be followed west a short distance to Haystack Lake. A day's hike from the lake takes you to the end of the logging road at Meachen Creek.

Typical slide/meadow crossing

Meachen Creek (I)
(east-west traverse of the range)

2 days round trip to Haystack Lake
Trail head to lake, 7 miles
Trail head 5,000 feet (1524 m)
Haystack Lake 6,200 feet (1890 m)

Approximately 4 miles (6 km) above St. Mary Lake, on the main road from Kimberley, Meachen Creek Road, the major branch, goes west. A good logging road crosses to the north side of the creek at about Mile 10 (16 km), and continues 13 miles (20 km) almost to the base of Snowcrest Mountain. Stay on the north side of the creek, picking up the trail at the road's end. Approximately 6 miles (9 km) and 3½ hours of hiking on a moderately brushy trail will get you to within a mile of Haystack Lake. Here the trail forks. On an open marshy area, the trail to the lake follows the left side of the creek. There is no trail around the lake and you will have to do a moderate amount of bushwhacking to reach the camping spots at the far end of the lake.

The main trail continues south along meadowland, then contours the slope at the headwaters of Kianuko Creek, ascending to a height of land south of Haystack through heavy forest and past several small lakes. This section of the trail is scheduled to be reopened by a BCFS crew.

Lockhart Creek (I)

2 days round trip
Trail head 2,000 feet (609 m)
Height of land 7,000 feet (2134 m)
Baker Lake 6,200 feet (1890 m)
Kaslo Topo

A reopened horse trail on Lockhart Creek provides access to the high country around Baker Lake and to the lake itself. A highlight of the trip is the meadow just below the lake where a perfectly carved meandering stream splits the meadow, creating a beautiful design.

At Lockhart Beach on Kootenay Lake, a trail sign is posted on the north side of Lockhart Creek, adjacent to Lockhart Beach Government Picnic Area. The trail follows the main creek, with two crossings (a single log for hikers and a shallow ford for horses). There is a sharp rise to the height of land, and a sharp drop to the meadow, which is still about three quarters of a mile this side of the lake. The distance from the trail head to the lake is 9 miles (14 km); allow about 7 hours on horseback, slightly more time on foot.

Camp can be made on the meadow or at the lake. There will be more mosquitoes on the meadow, but rougher turf at the lake. The meadows may be hard to cross at times because of marshy ground and ever-deepening ruts cut by horses' hoofs.

We have reports of hikers approaching Baker Lake via Akokli Creek. A logging road is followed into the headwaters of Akokli Creek, at which point the steep slopes directly above must be climbed without benefit of trail; then equally steep talus slopes dropping into the south end of the lake have to be negotiated.

Alpine area, western flank of Sphinx Mountain

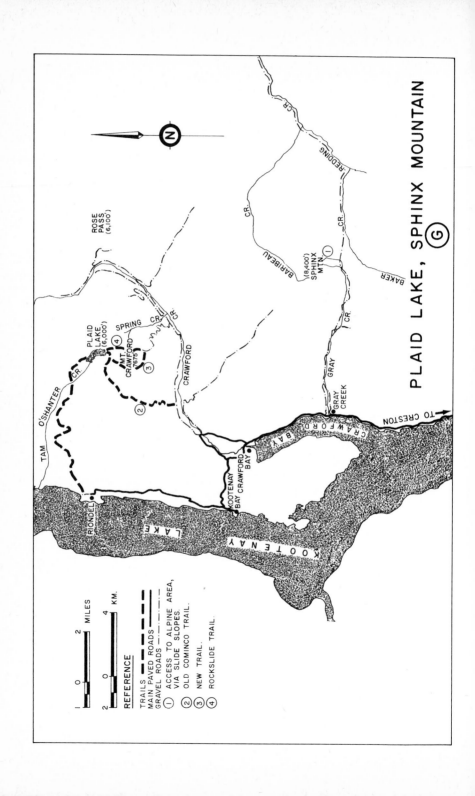

PLAID LAKE, SPHINX MOUNTAIN

G

REFERENCE
TRAILS
MAIN PAVED ROADS
GRAVEL ROADS

1 ACCESS TO ALPINE AREA, VIA SLIDE SLOPES.
2 OLD COMINCO TRAIL.
3 NEW TRAIL.
4 ROCKSLIDE TRAIL.

MILES
KM.

N

ROSE PASS (6,100')

PLAID LAKE (6,000')

SPRING CR.

MT. CRAWFORD 7675

TAM O'SHANTER CR.

CRAWFORD CR.

BARIBEAU CR.

(8,400') SPHINX MTN.

BAKER CR.

REDDING CR.

GRAY CR.

GRAY CREEK

RIONDEL

KOOTENAY LAKE

KOOTENAY BAY

CRAWFORD BAY

CRAWFORD BAY

TO CRESTON

Gray Creek (G)

Day trip
Gray Creek Pass 6,400 feet (1951 m)
Alpine area 7,500 feet (2286 m)
Kaslo Topo

A power line road connecting Gray Creek with Kimberley gives easy access to the alpine area in the vicinity of Sphinx Mountain, just above Gray Creek Pass.

The creek enters Kootenay Lake about 4 miles (6 km) north of the Gray Creek post office on Highway 3A. Take Oliver Road or Anderson Road to the pole line road, then follow it about 6 miles (9 km) to Gray Creek Pass. This is usually a four-wheel-drive road, but in dry summer conditions the steep upper sections of the road are passable to sturdy two-wheel-drive vehicles.

Leave your car near the pole line shack on the summit meadow and scramble up the open slope to the north where it has been cleared by successive avalanches. Within an hour you will be in the alpine basin beneath Sphinx Mountain, which is easily climbed via its southwest flank. The extensive alpine area spreads southeast, with excellent views of the most dominant peak in the southern Purcells—Snowcrest Mountain, 9,400 feet (3133 m).

This area is also accessible from the St. Mary side. Take the Redding Creek turnoff at Mile 19 on the main St. Mary Lake Road out of Kimberley (pole line road). In about 15 miles you will encounter a steep hill. The last couple of miles up to Gray Creek Pass should be attempted with two-wheel-drive vehicles in dry conditions only. The hike to the pass can be made in about an hour.

Crawford Creek (G)
(Plaid Lake)

Long day trip
Road head 2,000 feet (609 m)
Height of land 7,000 feet (2134 m)
Plaid Lake 5,800 feet (1768 m)
Kaslo Topo

There are four trails into this lake, which is situated in a recreational reserve at the head of Tam O'Shanter Creek. The most recent trail, completed in 1977, constitutes the quickest and easiest route. One trail exists on Tam O'Shanter Creek, but is a long and arduous hike from Riondel. An old Cominco pack trail leading up from a small sawmill near Washout Creek (a tributary of Crawford Creek) also is a long way—5 miles (8 km)—from the lake. A short but rough trail on the east flank of Mt. Crawford is to be superseded by a new trail on its west flank.

Access is by way of Crawford Creek, which is reached from Crawford Bay on Highway 3A. If you are coming from Gray Creek, take the first asphalt branch to the right (posted Crawford Creek Road); if you approach from the Kootenay Bay ferry, take the first paved road left past the Gulf station at Crawford Bay.

After a couple of miles, these two asphalt roads join to become the main gravel road on Crawford Creek. At Mile 8 (12 km), take the left fork of a road which ascends a hill, and at Mile 8.5 swing left again and follow a switchback road up through a clear-cut logging area. (This is an example of how your forest resource has been abused. Note the steep slopes, subsequent erosion and stream siltation—an obvious catastrophe.) If you come to a sign reading "Spring Creek" you have driven too far, so backtrack a few hundred yards to the only other road leading up the steep slopes.

The older trail begins at road's end; however, the new trail, one quarter mile short of road's end on the left, heads up the left side of the creek until a height of land is reached on the west flank of Mt. Crawford. The top end of the old Cominco trail comes in on the left near this point. The trail descends to the lake. Total walking time for the 2½ miles (4 km) should be about 2 hours, with an elevation gain of 1,000 feet (305 m).

If you prefer to travel away from man-made wasteland, the old Cominco trail is a reasonable alternative into the area. The trail head is less than 2 miles from the end of the asphalt, opposite a small sawmill operation.

Fry Creek Canyon (E)

Day trip
Road head 2,000 feet (609 m)
Trail head 2,000 feet (609 m)
Top end of trail 2,700 feet (823 m)
Lardeau Topo

This trip offers views of Kootenay Lake and the spectacular granite gorge at the lower end of Fry Creek. A recreational reserve has been placed on this part of Fry Creek.

From Highway 31, which passes through Kaslo and Argenta on the west side of Kootenay Lake, a gravel road branches east just south of Cooper Creek, 4 miles (6 km) north of Lardeau and in 4 miles (6 km) reaches the community of Argenta. Take the right branch of the road leading along the east side of the lake to Johnson's Landing, which consists of a community hall and a cluster of mailboxes. Drive alongside a cleared hillside, with a log house as landmark, until the road angles sharply left (.4 mile from Johnson's Landing). There is space enough for only two cars on the corner, so you may have to park elsewhere. Then prepare to search for the trail head.

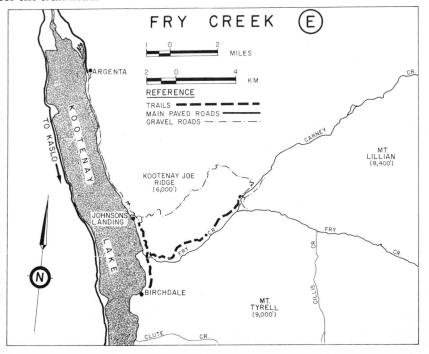

Make your way through trees on poorly defined trails for 200 yards (183 m), dropping slightly downhill and to the south, until you come to a small meadow. A skid road enters from the left. Follow it back up and left for 75 yards (68.5 m) until it intersects a graded trail heading south. There is supposed to be a trail register box here, but none was in evidence at the time of this writer's visit. A single strand of telephone wire follows the trail for 1½ miles (2.4 km) to the tiny settlement of Birchdale.

Three quarters of an hour of enjoyable hiking brings you to a decrepit bridge spanning the lower part of Fry Canyon. Do not cross. Fifty yards (45.7m) before the bridge, the Fry trail swings up the canyon and follows it without crossing the creek until, at the 6-mile (9 km) point, Carney Road is reached. Here a severely drooping logging bridge spans the creek. This is the point at which the Parks Branch trail crew stopped clearing, but fragments of the old Fry Creek trail still exist beyond here.

In some places the canyon trail is hewn across granite slabs, and new logs spanning the gaps (courtesy of the Parks Branch) make this a safe and rewarding day trip.

The Canyon views are most spectacular at the lower end; the upper part of the trail provides distant views of peaks to the east and the chance of seeing mountain goats on the rocky slopes.

Members of the Kootenay Mountaineering Club (aided by a helicopter) held a summer camp beside Bonny Gem Lake above Carney Road after the area had been scouted on foot by members.

Trail above Fry Creek delta on Kootenay Lake

Earl Grey Trail (D)
(to Toby Creek)

4 days one way
Hamill Creek 3,000 feet (914 m)
Earl Grey Pass 7,200 feet (2195 m)
Toby Creek 4,500 feet (1372 m)
Lardeau-Invermere Topo

A series of emergency shelters and tent platforms are located at points along the Earl Grey Trail. The trail is fairly well developed except at slide crossings, where you may have to hunt to find its continuation.

The Hamill Creek end of the Earl Grey Trail begins just to the north of the old mining community of Argenta at Kootenay Lake's north end. Follow the road that climbs up through the community (you are there as soon as you cross the Duncan River bridge: there are no streets or stores), to its end at the big Land Co-op gate. After another 1.5 miles, a sign on a left side road denotes the trail head. This side road goes for one half mile to a logging cut where cars can be left. The trail begins from the right lower corner of this cut, then switchbacks down to a bridge crossing Clint Creek.

The trail goes into Hamill valley proper, running along the bed of an old wagon road. Some bridging and corduroy sections remain. The trail makes its first creek crossing at a cable car built prior to 1920 on the site of an old bridge. Remember to leave the car hanging free so that hikers coming along the opposite side of the creek can retrieve it.

From here it is a short hike (about 3 hours) up to some old mine workings, a good camping spot with a large open area for tents.

A short walk from the mine workings brings you to a bridge by an old trapper's cabin. The first hiking trail, cut by the Opportunities for Youth crew in 1971, does not cross the creek but leaves from the cabin and goes up the bluffs. The trail was rerouted because of a fire that year, but it is still passable up to a fine lookout giving a view all the way up the valley to the headwall. Leave your packs at the cabin, for this is a one-hour side trip.

Across the bridge the trail goes through various ages of old burns. Successional forests of young cedar and hemlock and Douglas fir show how forests come back after fires. Cross the suspension bridge and continue along the lower part of a recent burn area for one third of a mile until you reach 7 Mile Camp (2½ hours from mine).

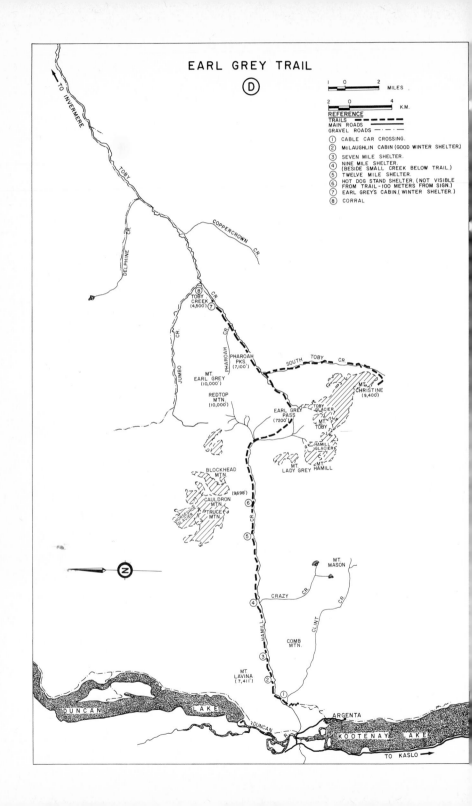

The whole valley from the cable bridge to 12 Mile Camp presents an unusually large climax stand of western hemlock and cedar. It is unusual for several reasons: its large size; its extreme age; the fact that it is one of the few stands undisturbed by roads, logging or mining. Through much of this forest there have been no fires for centuries, and some trees are nearly a thousand years old.

Between 7 Mile Camp and 9 Mile Camp (a 2½-hour hike) there is a creek crossing directly below a beaver dam. In high-water periods the foot logs may be underwater. If so, cross along the top of the dam.

The area from 9 Mile to 12 Mile is the end of the western hemlock zone which is characterized by western hemlock on the slopes and cedar, devil's club, and ferns on the flats along the creek.

Just below 12 Mile Camp there is a foot log crossing the creek and a ribbon-marked trail to a spectacular waterfall, visible (and audible) from the camp. Allow 30 minutes for this side trip.

The hike from 12 Mile to the Hotdog Stand (so named because of the shelter's design) takes you in about 4 hours into the lower subzone of Englemann spruce and sub-alpine fir. A closed tree canopy still shades the trail, but the forestation is less dense, the ground cover being white rhododendron and black mountain huckleberry. Watch for a sign on a tree: Hotdog's Last Stand, and follow the side trail north 100 yards.

After a couple of hours hiking from the Hotdog Stand, the bottom of the meadows—an area of spruce bog and sedge meadow—is reached. The Rockspike and the west side of Mt. Lady Grey can be seen on the right, and the headwall of the valley where the creek turns south is straight ahead. The trail along the north edge of the meadows leads to 21 Mile Camp.

Just up the slope from 21 Mile Camp is a waterfall which comes down through a narrow rock gorge. The falls and the view from there are well worth a visit, but no trail exists and it is necessary to bushwhack through the alder slide.

From 21 Mile to the north forks of Hamill Creek is an easy hike of less than an hour on a new, marked trail. Just past the forks the trail climbs steeply for about one quarter of a mile (½ km). Earl Grey Pass is about a mile and a half farther along on a gradually rising trail. At this point, it is about 8 miles to Toby Creek. (Transportation will be needed at the end.)

Cable car crossing on lower Hamill Creek

Camp on Toby Glacier moraine

Earl Grey Trail (D)
(from Invermere to Earl Grey Pass)

2 days round trip
Trail head 4,700 feet (I433 m)
Earl Grey Pass 7,200 feet (2195 m)
Lardeau Topo

From Invermere to Mineral King Mine the 20 miles (50 km) of road is used by logging and ore trucks. On weekdays it is possible to catch a ride, in either direction.

The Earl Grey Trail leaves the Mineral King Road at Jim MacKay's horse corral (see Toby Creek trail description) and goes across three open meadows divided by strips of pine forest. At the second of these open meadows is the cabin built for Governor-General Earl Grey in 1909. After the third meadow, Pharoah Creek is reached. From the corral to the creek will take about an hour.

The trail from Pharoah Creek to MacKay's Slide follows the creek bottom all the way except where it cuts up over a recent slide, and is an hour and a half hike.

At MacKay's Slide the trail turns at almost right angles to the creek and climbs to the top of the slide, then cuts through a thin belt of alder. From this point it maintains its elevation, following the contour around Redtop Mountain and Bannock Basin to a point above Toby Falls. The camp used by OFY study group in 1972 is located just before Toby Falls. This camp is suitable for use while there is snow run-off in the nearby creek, but by the first of August the creek is usually dry. It is a two-hour hike from the slide to the camp.

Above Toby Falls the trail starts climbing towards an outwash plain at the foot of Toby Glacier. The trail is well graded from the plain to Earl Grey Pass, with few switchbacks and a good view south. Two and a half hours should be allowed from the camp to the pass.

Glacier Creek (C)

Day trip
Trail head 5,200 feet (1585 m)
Jumbo Pass 7,200 feet (2195 m)
Glacier alpine area 5,300 feet (1615 m)
Lardeau Topo

This new logging road spearheads 16 miles (25 km) to the head of Glacier Creek's south fork, giving easy access to the hitherto remote ice field surrounding Truce and Cauldron mountains and passing within 2,000 feet (666 m) of Jumbo Pass. Also, a rough skid trail leads up the north fork of Glacier Creek to within striking distance of the Macbeth Icefield. And Fingerboard Peak is accessible from the head of Deep Creek, a tributary lower down on Glacier Creek.

Turn off Highway 31, as with the approach to Argenta, cross the Duncan River bridge, turn left (north) and drive alongside Duncan Lake until you cross Glacier Creek. On the north side of the bridge, the road turns east and heads up the creek valley.

In 5 miles (8 km) the first major tributary, Deep Creek, comes in from the south. At this point a rough skid road leads up Deep Creek; in 3 miles (4 km) it reaches a sub-alpine region below Fingerboard Peak.

The trail to Jumbo Pass, from near road's end, has long ago fallen into disuse; however, it is possible to find it on the upper alpine slopes above the heavy undergrowth near the road. A BCFS fire suppression crew has begun to clear this trail, and when the job is completed, the trail head will be posted. The trail ascends, with multiple switchbacks, from forest to alpine country.

At the north end of the pass is a four-man hut that was built in anticipation of helicopter skiing trips to the area. This excellent summer or winter shelter is left unlocked for the public's use.

From the pass, a newly cut hikers' trail descends steeply about 2 miles (3 km) to Jumbo Creek. The distance between Jumbo Creek Road and Glacier Creek Road is perhaps the shortest trail link of east and west drainages in the range.

Duncan River (general map)

Duncan Lake 1,892 feet (576 m)
Height of land 4,800 feet (1463 m)
Beaton Topo

As you proceed up the Duncan River, the creeks draining from the Purcells become shorter and shorter until a height of land is reached between the Duncan and Beaver rivers. At this point the Beaver flows north along the narrow corridor of the Purcell Trench, fed mainly by creeks from the Selkirk Range to the west, and enters the Columbia downstream from Donald on the Trans-Canada Highway.

Before the turn of the century, mining activity flourished along this narrow Purcell Trench, and mining camps such as Westfork (at the junction of the Westfall and Duncan rivers), and Placerville, Spender, Tenmile, and Circle City (in the neighbouring Duncan ranges of the Selkirks) were full of wide-eyed adventurers and fortune seekers. Although they pushed trails up most of the major drainages in this region, today few remain.

A main haul logging road reaches some 60 miles (96 km) from Lardeau to beyond Westfall Creek, with work taking place on Howser Creek and other side creeks. It is expected that this road will ultimately reach to the southern boundary of Glacier National Park.

Until enterprising woodspeople take it upon themselves to reopen some of the old trails in this northern part of the range, the country will remain inaccessible to the casual hiker, though it still holds attraction for the die-hard bushwhacker.

Kootenay Forest Products timber cruisers have informed us that the old trail up Howser Creek is in good condition for about 11 miles (17 km), and that there are several usable small cabins along the way. Up-to-date information on road conditions can be obtained from this company before starting out.

(top) *Headwaters of Fry Creek*; (bottom) *Commander Glacier*

Perry Creek (I)

Day trip
Road head 3,000 feet (914 m)
Ministry of Transport (MOT) site 7,000 feet (2134 m)
Richmond Lake 6,000 feet (1829 m)
Cranbrook-Kaslo-Creston Topo

The high country in the vicinity of Richmond Lake, the source of Perry Creek, can be reached by a short trail from the end of the main road, or by an easy two-day ridge walk along an undulating 7,000 feet (2134 m) ridge from the Ministry of Transport site on Puddingburn Mountain.

Not to be overlooked in this historic watershed is the former site of the huge wooden waterwheel that is now resident at Fort Steele; it stood beside Perry Creek just above Old Town. Traces of the heavy placer mining which took place around the turn of the century, and still takes place on sections of the creek, can be seen. Deserted cabins, hydraulic nozzles, a railway steam shovel and caved-in shafts lie in disarray amid the jack pine forest.

The Perry Creek Road turnoff is a quarter of a mile south of the Wycliffe bridge across the St. Mary River on Highway 95 between Cranbrook and Kimberley.

At Mile 6 (9 km), just before reaching a cluster of old buildings known as Old Town, the main road crosses a creek and continues another 4 miles (6 km) to the Ministry of Transport (MOT) turnoff on the right. The road ends 15 miles (24 km) farther, just below Richmond Lake.

MOT Ridgewalk (I)
(MOT to Richmond Lake)

2 days one way (approximately 10 miles to lake)
MOT site 7,000 feet (2134 m)
Richmond Lake 6,000 feet (1829 m)
Cranbrook-Kaslo-Creston Topo

From the MOT turnoff (see Perry Creek, p. 61) drive another 6 miles
(9 km) to the MOT site on top of Puddingburn Mountain. From here, a
jeep road follows the ridge crest west for 5 miles (8 km). The road may be
too rough for your vehicle, but it is an enjoyable hike. From the road's
end, near Hoot Lake, you have to find your own way along the barren
ridge, traversing 8,174-foot Grassy Mountain, which is midway to Richmond Lake. Great views can be had into the head of Hellroaring Creek
and the main St. Mary valley beyond. From ridge's end, descend to Richmond Lake, where a trail from the southeast end of the lake leads down to
the road and, hopefully, a pickup vehicle.

Richmond Lake (I)

Day trip (see Perry Creek trail description)
Cranbrook-Kaslo-Creston Topo

From the road's end on the north side of Perry Creek, a narrow skid road
angles up the hill beside the creek and leads to a steep trail on the upper
slopes. This takes you to the one-square-mile lake in about an hour. A
smaller lake shares the sub-alpine setting with Richmond, and is a five-
minute walk from the creek inlet at the north end.

A simple log crossing

ST. MARY VALLEY AREA (H)

Kaslo-Cranbrook Topo

The St. Mary River, along with the Spillimacheen and Skookumchuck rivers, is one of the longest in the Purcells, being more than 50 miles (80 km) from headwaters to the point where it exits the range.

Its main valley also holds the range's largest body of water, 10-square-mile St. Mary Lake. On a high plateau at its headwaters lies the 21-square-mile St. Mary Alpine Park, containing more than 30 alpine lakes. The south end of the Purcell Wilderness Conservancy borders on this park and includes the headwaters of the main St. Mary River and of Dewar Creek, a major tributary.

Because of easy access, the valley bottoms of most of these drainages are heavily laced with logging roads. The West Kootenay Power and Light power line road from Kimberley to Gray Creek via St. Mary River, Redding Creek, and Gray Creek is the only road linking the East and West Kootenay through the main body of the range.

The St. Mary turnoff is 300 yards (274 m) north of Marysville on Highway 95. St. Mary Lake is reached at Mile 11 (17 km). Other distances are: Meachen Creek turnoff, 15 miles (24 km); Redding Creek turnoff, 19 miles (30 km); end of Dewar Creek, 40 miles (64 km); end of White Creek—edge of Alpine Park—42 miles (67 km); end of St. Mary Road, 43 miles (68 km); Gray Creek Pass, 48 miles (76 km).

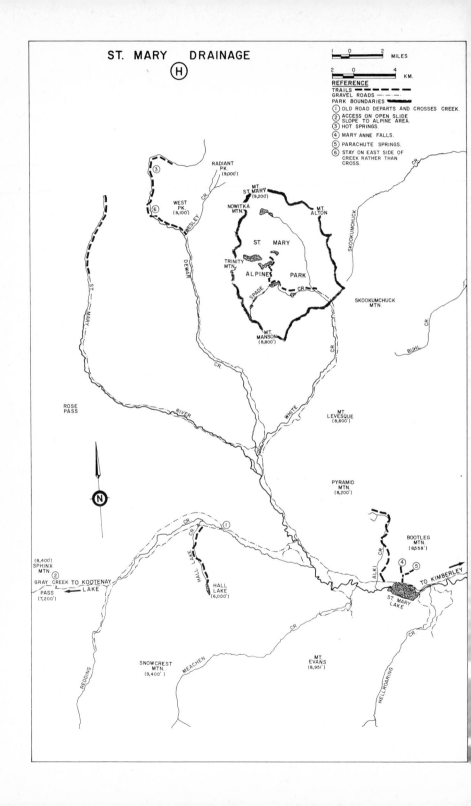

Mary Anne Falls (H)

Half-day trip
1 mile (1.6 km)
Trail head 3,200 feet (975 m)
Falls 4,700 feet (1433 m)
Kaslo-Cranbrook Topo

This trail offers a delightful half-day hike, giving good views of St. Mary valley as well as leading to the falls on Argyle Creek.

There is parking space on a sharp corner at the north end of St. Mary Lake by a group of cabins. (A sign on one says "Musser's Cabin.") Hike up the short, steep skid road to a pole line, then climb obliquely left for 200 yards (183 m) until a blaze at the upper edge of the pole line denotes the start of the trail.

Midway to the falls, watch for a sign (on a blackened tree trunk) indicating a trail on the right which offers a side trip to Parachute Springs. The springs are about equidistant from the falls at this fork. If the trail to the falls is washed out, following the creek bed will bring you to their base.

Hall Lake, Redding Creek (H)

Long day trip
Hall Lake 5,000 feet (1524 m)
Trail head 4,000 feet (1219 m)
Kaslo-Cranbrook Topo

This picturesque sub-alpine lake teems with pan-size trout.

At Mile 4.5 from main St. Mary Road, turn onto a new logging road and drop down to 5 Mile Camp (Cominco shack), cross the bridge over Redding Creek, and proceed 2 miles (3 km) to the Hall Creek bridge. Park on its south side and pick up the trail 100 yards back, just above the main road. At first, the trail crosses benchland and then follows the streambed with two crossings. The 3 miles (4 km) to the lake can be covered in about 3 hours. There are camping spots at the north end of the lake.

St. Mary River (H)

1-2 days round trip
Trail head 4,600 feet (1402 m)
Basin head 5,400 feet (1646 m)
Kaslo-Cranbrook Topo

An outfitter's trail follows the broad floor of the St. Mary River main branch through particularly fine open stands of spruce on the upper reaches of the valley.

Leave your car at Mile 43 (end of St. Mary Road out of Marysville) and follow the trail up the east side of the river to open grassy slopes at the head of the valley. A lovely alpine lake is tucked into a pocket at the head of the valley and is easy to reach by ascending the barren slopes of an avalanche path for 1,500 feet (457 m) on the west side of the basin. Stay close to a gushing rivulet until it peters out, then head diagonally to the right. In several hundred feet you will reach the lake.

(left) *Mary Anne Falls*; (below) *Meadow, upper reaches of St. Mary River*

Dewar Creek (H)
(Hot Springs)

1-2 days round trip
Kaslo-Cranbrook Topo

From the main St. Mary Road turn right at Mile 27 and drive 13 miles to road's end. In 5 miles an outfitter's trail passes a small natural hot springs. The formation of the springs is such that you need to use some ingenuity if you are to find a method of bathing in them comfortably. They are scalding hot at their source and tepid by the time the water trickles into the creek a hundred feet below.

Cross Wesley Creek on a log or, in low water, ford the creek and pick up the trail on the other side. Follow it along the east side of the valley bottom until it crosses Dewar Creek. Rather than ford the creek here, bushwhack along the bank on game trails until you pick up the outfitter's trail which crosses back at this point. As the trail approaches the hot spring formations beside Dewar Creek, be wary of many misleading game trails coming onto the main trail. If you have bypassed the hot springs, you will soon come to a sharp eastward bend in the valley, and it is only a short hike back to them.

Looking down Parker Creek valley to Redding Creek

Meachen Creek (see Sanca Creek)

Sphinx Mountain (see Gray Creek Pass)

Alki Creek (H)
(Bill Murphy Memorial Trail)

Long day trip
Trail head 3,700 feet (1128 m)
Alki/Matthews Pass 7,600 feet (2317 m)
Kaslo Topo

A mining trail was recently reopened to the height of land between Alki and Matthew creeks by a team of Kimberley students. It is a pleasant, long day's trip into a couple of sub-alpine lakes and old mine workings.

As the main St. Mary Road approaches Alki Creek, just north of St. Mary Lake, a clear-cut logging road turns right (east) and winds across the bare hillside for one quarter of a mile. From the road's end, the trail begins and rounds a flank of Bootleg Mountain, then rises slightly to follow a high contour above the creek until it reaches the first set of mine workings at creek level, at Mile 2.5 (4 km). Above this, the trail crosses the main creek several times on its way to old workings just below the Alki/Matthews pass. At this point it is possible to wander about in the high benches and alongside several tarns.

Mountain goats

St. Mary Alpine Park (H)

Multi-day trip (alpine area, 1-2 days round trip)
Trail head (end of White Creek Road) 5,400 feet (1391 m)
Spade Lake 6,400 feet (1646 m)
Huggard Lake 7,000 feet (2134 m)
Kaslo Topo

There are no established trails giving access to St. Mary Alpine Park. Start on St. Mary Road; turn right onto White Creek Road at Mile 24.5 (39.4 km) and follow it over two bridges for 9.5 miles (15.3 km) to a washed-out bridge. (The detour around this impass is negotiable by four-wheel drive.) Three miles (4.8 km) from this point by road is the junction of Spade Creek and White Creek. Park your vehicle here, if you are not already on foot. Proceed left across Spade Creek, following an old logging road on the left (south) side of the creek to Spade Lake. Cross to the north side of the lake at the outlet and follow a game trail to the west end of the lake. The route into the upper lakes climbs the steep slope between two streams to Huggard Lake, 1,500 feet (457 m) above. It is a difficult bushwack through bog, alder and devil's club, and some cliff-scaling is necessary, but a fit and determined hiker can traverse this section in two hours. Once you reach the open alpine larch parkland at Huggard Lake, the going becomes considerably easier. Travel among the high lakes is very easy with the aid of a topographical map.

Totem Lake and peak, St. Mary Alpine Park

Skookumchuck Creek (general map)

Day trip
Kaslo-Cranbrook Topo

A number of day trips can be made into this area. It is worth exploring if you are willing to do some bushwhacking.

Take the turnoff on Highway 93/95 to the Skookumchuck pulp mill and continue past it to the railway side of Torrent. The road branches left, swinging up the Skookumchuck valley, ascending a low mountain, and dropping into Sandown Creek valley. Four miles (6 km) past Sandown there is a washout on the road, which in dry conditions can be driven around. A mile past this is a shallow ford, also navigable in good weather. The road branches left to Buhl Creek at Mile 22 (35 km). The main road continues up the main river to Greenland Creek, which it follows for less than 2 miles (3 km) to old mine workings known as "Pico City."

Basin, top end of Findlay Creek

Findlay Creek (F)

Multi-day trip
Trail head 3,800 feet (1158 m)
Trail end 5,800 feet (1768 m)
Lardeau Topo

The as yet roadless valleys of Findlay and Dutch creeks contain two of the longest passable trails in the range, after the Earl Grey Trail.

The Findlay is the most northerly Purcell drainage to empty its water into the Kootenay River, which it does near Canal Flats. The remoteness of the peaks discourages climbers. From mountains Morigeau and Findlay at the north end of the Findlay Glacier to Radiant Peak at the top end of Toby Creek there is much to occupy the hiker and climber.

A road exists on the lower part of Findlay; it is reached by turning off Highway 93/95 at the Thunder Hill campground, just above the south end of Columbia Lake.

Follow the road for 17 miles (28 km). At its end, the trail continues on the north side of the creek for another 25 miles (40 km). A good camp-site, which can be reached in two long days of hiking, is found at the head of Morigeau Creek.

At the last acute bend of Findlay Creek, Granite Creek joins the main stream and drains a large glacier on the east flanks of Mt. Morigeau and Mt. Findlay immediately south of Trikootenay Peak. (This glacier is also accessible from the head of Dutch Creek.) The head of Granite Creek can be reached from the Morigeau campsite by heading southeast across the ridge of Mt. Findlay and descending past a large lake.

The ultimate source of Findlay Creek is in the snowfields on the north side of Mt. St. Mary. There are no passes in the upper reaches of Findlay Creek that are suitable for travel with horses, should you take them into the Fry, St. Mary, or Skookumchuck basins.

Of particular interest to the backpaper are the beautiful falls on Morigeau Creek, and the meadowland of upper Findlay Creek.

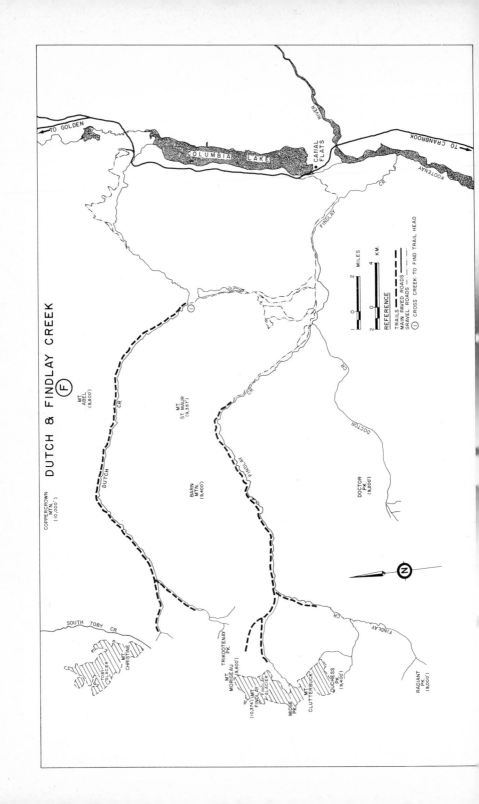

Dutch Creek (F)
(source of the Columbia River)

Multi-day trip
Trail head 3,800 feet (1158 m)
Trail end 6,000 feet (1829 m)
Lardeau Topo

This drainage is an alternate route of access to the peaks in the northern end of the Findlay group and also to the head of Carney Creek and the south fork of Toby Creek.

Most people on horseback start the trail up Dutch Creek at the Hawke Ranch, 4 miles west of Fairmont Hot Springs. Backpackers may begin farther up the creek at the end of a road which passes Whitetail Lake. Begin as with the approach to Findlay Creek and turn north (right) off Findlay Road at Mile 7 (11 km), driving up Deer Creek past Whitetail Lake and into the lower part of Dutch Creek valley.

The trail is located on the north side of the creek, and a crossing must be found to get to it. From here it is possible to reach the head of Dutch Creek in two days, though in the upper portions of the valley the trail is vague and the ground swampy. As with the Findlay trail, it is about 25 miles (37 km) to the head of Dutch Creek valley.

For the most part, the route follows the north and west sides of the valley. At the end of the first day, a good campsite can be made beside a decrepit forestry cabin, southeast of Coppercrown Mountain, where a large cascade occurs in the stream. One mile upstream, Dutch Creek makes an acute bend south for 8 miles to its terminal forks below Saffron Peak. The south fork has its origin in a 3- to 4-square-mile glacial basin which is the ultimate source of the Columbia River. This area was first mapped by J. M. Thorington in 1930.

Immediately south of Saffron Peak a low wooded pass, at 6,800 feet (2073 m), with a summit tarn leads across the main watershed from a branch of Dutch Creek to Carney Creek. This is the lowest crossing of the range between the Dogtooths and the head of St. Mary River. The south fork of Toby Creek can be reached by dropping slightly into the top end of Carney Creek and heading north for 3 miles (4 km) to a pass between the two creeks.

TOBY CREEK AREA (D)

(See individual elevations)
Lardeau Topo

The logging roads at Toby, Horsethief, Frances, and Bugaboo creeks penetrate to some of the most spectacular groups of peaks and glaciers in the range. This area has traditionally attracted the attention of climbers, one of the most famous being Austrian climbing guide Conrad Kain, who settled in Wilmer, within horse packing and snowshoeing distance of these drainages.

At the top end of Toby Creek, the Earl Grey Trail provides a link with the West Kootenay (see Hamill Creek trail description); the south fork of Toby leads into the alpine area south of Toby Glacier; and at Jumbo and Delphine creeks, roads have been pushed to within easy reach of the high country. A road also leads up to the eastern side of Mt. Nelson and the deserted buildings of Paradise Mine.

Approach Invermere from Highway 93; pass through Athalmer, and, once across the train tracks, turn right. In one mile the road crosses Toby Creek, and Toby Road runs left just north of the crossing.

As you proceed up the valley, you will pass a road leading to the Paradise Mine at the old Jackpine mill site at Mile 10 (16 km). Panorama Ski Hill will be on your left at Mile 10.5 (16.8 km); Delphine Creek Road on your right at Mile 16 (25 km); Jumbo Creek Road, Mineral King Mine dump and a horse corral on your right, all around Mile 25 (40 km).

Stream crossing, Morigeau Creek

South Fork of Toby Creek (D)

Multi-day trip
Trail head 4,700 feet (1433 m)
Height of land 7,500 feet (2286 m)
Lardeau Topo

Begin as for the Earl Grey Trail, at the horse corral at road's end. At Mile 6 (9 km), the trail branches south (left) as you come within sight of the falls on Toby Creek. When you reach a ford on the creek where an outfitter's cabin is to be seen on the other side, walk upstream until you find a log crossing.

From the cabin, there are 8 miles (12 km) of continuous creek crossings along this south fork of Toby Creek to the alpine area south of Toby Glacier. You can look down into the headwaters of Dutch and Carney creeks from this height of land.

Jumbo Creek (D and C)

Day trip
Maximum elevation of road 5,700 feet (1737 m)
Lardeau Topo

After crossing Jumbo Creek, and just before the Mineral King Mine buildings on the main Toby Creek Road, Jumbo Creek Road branches right (north), and climbs for 21 miles (19 km) to the head of the creek. There are a couple of shallow fords along the way which are manoeuvrable by vehicles with good clearance.

Approximately 9 miles (14 km) from Toby Creek, a newly blazed trail climbs steeply to Jumbo Pass, on the west side of the road. Access to the snowfield near Glacier Dome and the back sides (south slopes) of the peaks surrounding Lake of the Hanging Glacier is possible from the end of the Jumbo Creek road.

The Pharoah Peaks; Earl Grey Pass, left centre

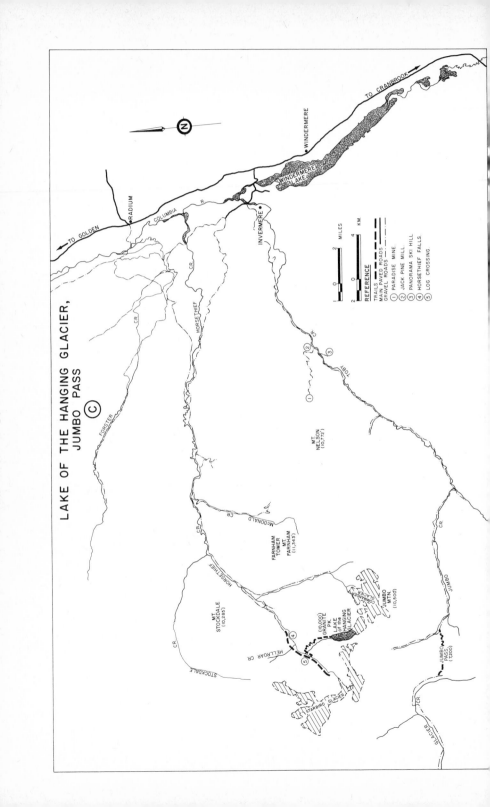

LAKE OF THE HANGING GLACIER,
JUMBO PASS ©

Horsethief Drainage (C)

Day trip
Road's end 6,000 feet (1829 m)
Lake of the Hanging Glacier 8,500 feet (2581 m)
Starbird Glacier 6,700 feet (2042 m)
Invermere Topo

This trail features spectacular Lake of the Hanging Glacier, Starbird Glacier, and Commander Glacier, and the greatest concentration of lofty summits in the interior ranges. In 1807 David Thompson gave Mt. Nelson its name; Farnham Tower was the block seen from Mt. Sugarloaf in the Selkirks by Forster, Huber, and Topham in 1890.

For access to Lake of the Hanging Glacier and Starbird Glacier, take a logging road which passes through the sawmill grounds at Radium. This road crosses the Columbia at Mile 2 (3 km); crosses West Side Road at Mile 7 (11 km); McDonald Creek at Mile 22 (35 km); the bridge to Farnham Creek at Mile 30 (48 km). The road ends at Mile 36 (57 km). (Note: Because of a recent closure of the Radium West Side Road, access is best via Invermere-West Side Road, though the logging road may be reopened at any time.) From the road's end to Lake of Hanging Glacier is 5 miles (8 km); to Starbird Glacier, 4 miles (6 km).

Starbird Pass

From road's end, a five-minute walk along the main creek through thick underbrush affords a view of the impressive Horsethief Creek falls, which can be heard from afar but cannot actually be seen clearly until you have bushwhacked to their base.

A skid road ascends obliquely up the slope from the road's end to small Hellroar Creek which can be crossed on logs. An excellent trail leads up through magnificent stands of spruce to benchlands along Horsethief Creek. Hike along the flats until you come to a horse crossing. Do not cross at this point, but follow the north bank of the creek for a short distance until you come to a couple of logs spanning the creek. Cross here and return on the south bank until you pick up the trail. The trail at first leads left for 300 feet (100 m), then switchbacks steeply up the east (left) side of Lake of the Hanging Glacier Creek and leads into an alpine area just below the lake.

Because of the delicate nature of the lake shore, do not camp at this end but pick a site either on the more robust meadows beside the trail on the approach to the lake or on the grassy benches above and to the west of the lake.

A number of day trips are possible from this campsite, one being a hike down the east side of the lake for a close look at the 150-foot (50 m) wall of ice entering the lake's other end. Another hike can be made up the slopes of Glacier Dome for a good view of the lake and the sea of mountains stretching away to the north.

Starbird Glacier View (C)

Invermere Topo

Begin as with the Lake of the Hanging Glacier trail, but instead of crossing Horsethief Creek on the logs, continue along the north bank on game trails for 2 miles (3 km) until you reach a steep-sided valley at the head of the creek. At this point you will have a good view of the glacier tongue and the rolling waters of the newly born creek. It is not advisable to proceed to the base of the glacier unless the slopes are absolutely dry, as this section, though short, is hazardous.

Lake of the Hanging Glacier and Glacier Dome

Farnham Creek (C)

Half and full day trips
Invermere Topo

For access to Commander Glacier and its basin at the head of the creek, turn left off the main Horsethief Creek road at Mile 30 (48 km) and cross the bridge. The logging road up Farnham Creek is passable for ordinary vehicles for approximately 4 miles, and there is excellent camping at this point. The valley forks just above here, with skid roads leading 2 miles (3 km) to the alpine area at the head of Farnham Creek (south).

McDonald Creek (C)

Day trips
Invermere Topo

At Mile 22 (35 km) from Radium, a private mining road turns south off the main Horsethief Creek road, up McDonald Creek. After following this creek for about 5 miles (8 km), the road swings up the tributary, Red Line Creek, which it follows for another couple of miles into a basin beneath Red Line Peak. There are mine workings and old roads leading up to them both near the junction of the two creeks and at the head of Red Line. From the workings, bare talus slopes lead up to open ridges which afford fine views of the Farnham Group.

Forster Creek (C)

2-3 days round trip
Trail head 5,000 feet (1524 m)
Whirlpool Lake 7,000 feet (2134 m)
Invermere Topo

A logging road pushes almost 21 miles (33 km) from Radium into the headwaters of Forster Creek. Proceed as with the Horsethief Creek approach; about a mile and a half after you cross West Side Road, a sign shows the Forster Creek Road swinging off to the northwest (right). Follow this road to a washout at Mile 21 (33 km) and continue to hike 6 or 7 miles (10 km) to meadow camping below Whirlpool and Thunderwater lakes. The high glaciated area around the lakes lends itself to exploration by experienced hikers.

Block towers

Frances Creek (C)
(Upper Dunbar Lakes)

1-2 days round trip
Trail head 7,000 feet (2134 m)
Mine workings 7,500 feet (2286 m)
Pass 9,400 feet (2864 m)
Invermere Topo

Nine miles (14 km) from West Side Road, a road forks right (north) off
Frances Creek Road and continues for 2 miles (3 km) up to the Steel Group
of mine workings at 7,500 feet (2286 m). Staying on the left flank of two
prominent peaks to the north of the workings, make your way on semi-
open slopes to a pass at 9,400 feet (2864 m). Hiking time to the pass is
about 2½ hours. From here, follow a gently sloping glacier down to the
cluster of lakes.

Starbird Glacier terminus

The Bugaboos, from the alpine above Chalice Creek

BUGABOOS (B)

Invermere Topo

William Putnam's *Climber's Guide to the Interior Ranges of B.C.* describes the Bugaboo Group as "... one of the most spectacular mountain groups in Canada, not great in extent, but surprising in the sheerness of its [granite] spires. The group generally affords climbing of more technical character than do most other peaks of the Interior Ranges, or, in fact, of the Rockies." He goes on to say: "Conrad Kain (1883-1934) considered Bugaboo Spire to have been his alltime most difficult ascent, and admitted that Snowpatch Spire (unclimbed until 1940) was beyond his powers."

Leave Highway 95 at Brisco, follow a gravel road across railway tracks for one quarter of a mile, and turn right at a sawmill. The road spans the Columbia River and after a couple of miles it crosses the West Side Road. At approximately Mile 25 (40 km) there is a turnoff to Chalice Creek; at Mile 26 (41 km) another turnoff leads to Bugaboo Lodge with access to Bugaboo Spires and Cobalt Lake; the main road follows Bugaboo Creek south to a jeep road leading up to Bugaboo Pass.

89

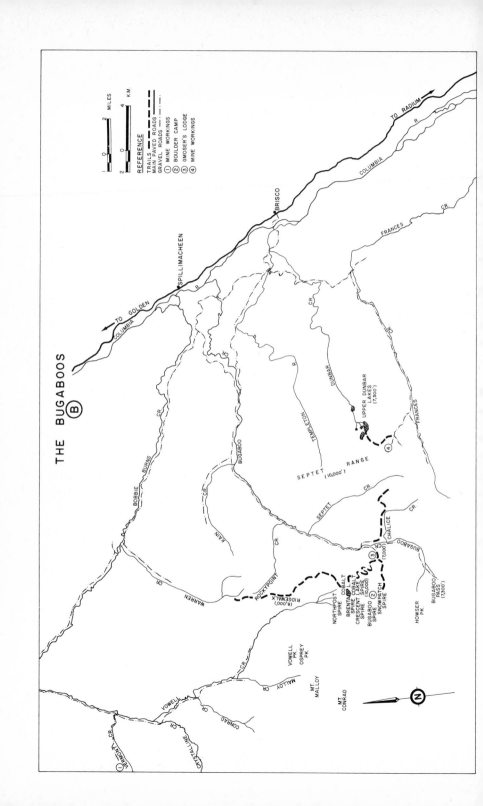

Cobalt Lake (B)

Long day trip
Lodge 4,900 feet (1494 m)
Lake 7,640 feet (2330 m)
Invermere Topo

Nestled between Northpost and Cobalt Lake Spire, Cobalt Lake is a strenuous but rewarding day hike from Hans Gmoser's Bugaboo Lodge, which is located on a tributary of Bugaboo Creek 27 miles (43 km) from Brisco, on Highway 93.

Leave your car at the lodge parking lot and proceed to the base of a fairly recent forest fire burn (above the man-made lake) to a sign reading "Blue Lake" (Cobalt Lake). Approximately 2,000 feet (609 m) of climbing on a trail brings you to the height of land. Then make your way across undulating alpine ground to the lake. This involves 2½ miles (4 km) and 3 to 4 hours of hiking from the lodge.

Optional: Should you have two or more days to spare, a couple of loop trips from the lodge offer an attractive extension to the Cobalt Lake hike. After you reach the height of land, rather than heading immediately to the lake, take the ridge which leads north, separating the Bugaboo and Vowell creek drainages. The continuous ridge can be followed to the head of Rocky Point Creek, 6 miles (9 km) from Cobalt Lake, or to Warren Creek, 12 miles (19 km). Old roads in these drainages can be followed down to Bugaboo Creek and Bobbie Burns Creek respectively. If you want to leave a second car for pickup, consult the B.C. Forest Service at Spilimacheen to find out how far the roads are driveable. Because of the heavy snow pack on these routes, the two- to three- day trip would be best made in mid- to late summer.

Cobalt Lake can also be reached from Boulder Camp (see next description).

A peak beyond Chalice Creek in the Septet Group

Aftermath of midsummer snowstorm, Boulder Camp

Boulder Camp (B)

Day trip
Trail head 4,900 feet (1494 m)
Boulder Camp 7,700 feet (2155 m)
Invermere Topo

High above the west fork of Bugaboo Creek, under Snowpatch Spire, is Conrad Kain Hut, which was built by the Alpine Club of Canada to accommodate 80 persons. It is now maintained by the B.C. Parks Branch in 1.2-mile square Bugaboo Glacier Provincial Park. A good trail from the end of the newly repaired road from Hans Gmoser's lodge leads up to the camp in less than 3 miles (4 km), about a 3-hour hike.

You may pay a small fee and stay at the hut, or camp on gravel flats one half mile above Boulder Camp, near the base of Bugaboo Spire. Anyone proceeding onto the ice fields beyond Boulder Camp should carry a rope and have some knowledge of glacier travel.

Chalice Creek (B)

Day trip
Trail head 5,000 feet (1524 m)
Chalice Creek meadow 6,100 feet (1859 m)
Alpine meadows 7,500 feet (2286 m)
Invermere Topo

Another nice hike, with a superb distant view of the Bugaboos, is the
Chalice Creek trail, built especially for hikers by a youth employment
project team in 1972. Just before the main Bugaboo road swings up the
main fork of Bugaboo Creek, near Gmoser's lodge, a new logging road
crosses the creek to the south and climbs a hillside above the south side
of the creek. After about 1.5 miles (2.5 km) look for a sign marker on the
left denoting the start of the trail. It takes you to the alpine area in less
than half a day of pleasant hiking, passing Chalice Creek meadow; once
on top you can find several sources of drinking water, including tarns.
The craggy peaks of the Septet Group rise directly east of here.

The non-climbing recreationist who comes to the Bugaboo area to fish,
hike and explore will be offended by the sloppy logging practices and subsequent erosion and siltation of Bugaboo Creek. No better are the gouges
left on Bugaboo Pass by a probing D8 cat performing mineral exploration
or the obliteration on Chalice Creek of a section of hikers' trail which has
been pre-empted by uncontrolled slash burning on the adjacent logging
site.

This sort of resource mismanagement is not unique to this part of the
range, but it is the most distressingly graphic example of blatant disregard
by resource planners for an area of unusually rich mountain scenery and
recreational potential.

Spillimacheen River Area (B)

1 or more days round trip
Vermont Creek trail head 5,400 feet (1646 m)
Vowell Creek trail head 5,500 feet (1676 m)
Invermere-Golden Topo

The largest drainage in the entire range, though probably the least visited, is the Spillimacheen River. The river and its tributaries drain from the remote northern reaches into the Columbia River near the community bearing the same name.

Mountaineers and glacier hikers are drawn to the Vowell Group, whose massive ice field flows north from the Bugaboos. Access is across the Glacier from the Bugaboo-Snowpatch col, or from the marshy valley of Vowell Creek.

High country may be reached via an active mine road on Vermont Creek or an old mine road on McMurdo Creek, as well as an old pack trail into the basin at the head of Crystalline Creek.

Leave the highway at Spillimacheen, cross the Columbia River, and turn left on West Side Road. After half a mile, turn right onto Bobbie Burns Road and follow it up to the junction of Bobbie Burns Creek and the Spillimacheen River. Spillimacheen Road turns right here and crosses the river, following its north side to a point upstream from McMurdo Creek. From here a rough road leads 7 miles (11 km) into meadows and an alpine basin at the head of McMurdo Creek. The small Spillimacheen Glacier squats at the 8,000 foot (2438 m) level above the basin.

The main Bobbie Burns Road adjoins the Vowell Creek Road at Mile 17 (27 km), and swings up Vowell Creek almost to its headwaters at Mile 42 (65 km). On the upper reaches, the road is passable only in dry conditions.

At Mile 33 (52 km) on the Vowell Creek Road, a recently renovated road heads up Vermont Creek to old mine workings. A trail which begins across the valley to the northwest of the workings leads to the height of land.

Along Malloy Creek, the uppermost tributary of Vowell Creek, a new road which turns off Vowell Creek Road at Mile 41.5 leads to semi-open terrain which can be hiked for 3 miles (4 km) to the base of the steep glacier of Osprey Peak. Access to the Vowell Group is easier via the Vowell Creek Road.

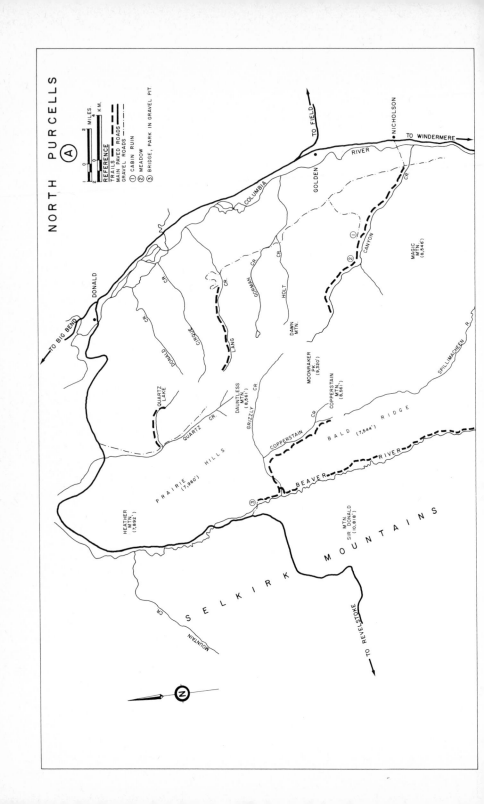

NORTHERN PURCELLS (A)

This portion of the range, from the headwaters of the Spillimacheen River north to the terminus at the confluence of the Beaver and Columbia rivers, is noted for its large population of alders and grizzlies.

The easternmost border of Glacier National Park reaches into the top of the Grizzly and Copperstain creek drainages, then runs along the crest of the Purcell Trench to the start of Duncan River. In this area there are two park trails, one along the Beaver River valley bottom, one in the Copperstain Creek valley. Both are maintained by the Park Warden Service, though rain and undergrowth can contribute to a soggy, boggy journey in either drainage.

The potential for ridge walks in the central and eastern section of the range is good. Parties have linked portions of old mining trails together, utilizing open ridges wherever possible, to traverse from Canyon Creek to the Beaver River on multi-day excursions.

Icebound lake, head of St. Mary River

Canyon Creek (A)

2-3 days round trip
Trail head 5,500 feet (1676 m)
Height of land 7,200 feet (2195 m)
Golden Topo

This valley provides a refuge for a variety of big game animals, including mountain goat, elk, and bear. The trail is relatively good for the first 7 miles (11 km), but then becomes steeper and plows through underbrush to terminate after 12 miles (19 km) in the high country at the foot of Moonraker Peak.

From Nicholson, a cluster of farmhouses 5 miles (8 km) south of Golden on Highway 95, drive west on a good gravel road for 8 miles (12 km), passing Cedar Lake on the left. A sign on the left, "Canyon Creek Fire Access Road," denotes the start of a rough, 4-mile-long road which leads up to the northern slope, dropping into the canyon on the creek. Many people walk this section rather than risk injuring their vehicle.

From road's end the trail angles down towards the creek, then continues all the way up the right (north) side of the creek to its end. At approximately Mile 6 (9 km), you pass the ruins of a log cabin and at Mile 7 (11 km) come to a broad meadow which is ideally suited to camping. This can be reached in less than a day and is a good starting point for the next day's climb.

Although much of this trail's attraction lies in its lower section, access to the high country is possible by continuing on a slightly overgrown trail for another day's hike into the Moonraker Basin.

Quartz Creek (A)

Day trip
Trail head 4,000 feet (1219 m)
Lake 6,400 feet (1951 m)
Glacier Park Topo

This trail offers a nice day trip into Quartz Lake, which is a popular destination of local fishermen. The sub-alpine slopes above the lake and a small icebound lake with a nice view of the ranges to the north invite the overnight hiker.

The Quartz Creek logging road leaves Highway 1 (the Trans-Canada) 26 miles west of Golden, on the left (south) side of the highway. If you drive across the Quartz Creek bridge on the highway, you have gone too far; drive back less than a mile.

Drive up the logging road, conditions permitting, for 3 miles (4 km) to the first major creek crossing. Park on the other side of the bridge. Backtrack a few hundred yards and climb a clay bank. You will find the start of the trail on a bench 30 to 40 feet (9-12 m) above the road. From here into the lake, a distance of 3 miles (4 km), the trail is clearly defined.

The trail climbs fairly steeply for most of its length and stays on the left side of the creek until a rock slide is reached just below the lake. Continue on the left side or cross onto the rock slide and contour around to the lake.

BEAVER RIVER AND
COPPERSTAIN CREEK AREA (A)

Note: this area is part of a national park, and overnight hikers must register with the Park Warden Service on Rogers Pass. There is no trail register at the East Park Gate. Up-to-date trail information can be obtained from the wardens.

Beaver River (A)

3 or more days round trip
Trail head 3,000 feet (914 m)
Headwaters 4,600 feet (1402 m)
Glacier Park Topo

This 26-mile (41 km) trail follows the Purcell Trench through stands of heavy timber and many marshy areas. The trail is used by the park wardens for patrols. It originally connected with the Duncan River trail and was used during early mining activity. Views are somewhat limited by the timber and the steep-sided valleys. From the Trans-Canada Highway as you travel east the access road turns off 7 miles (11 km) past the Warden's Service Office on Rogers Pass; 5 miles (8 km) west of the East Park Gate, if you are coming from Golden.

A mile-long road crosses the Beaver River and ends at a gravel pit on the left (east) side of the river. The trail begins here and stays on the left side of the river, crossing Grizzly Creek at Mile 4 (6 km) on a footbridge. The worst of the boggy sections is encountered at Mile 14 (22 km). There are numerous meadows suitable for camping along the way.

Copperstain Creek (A)

2-3 days round trip
Trail head 3,000 feet (914 m)
Headwaters 7,000 feet (2134 m)
Glacier Park Topo

At the headwaters of Copperstain Creek lie one of the most scenic alpine and sub-alpine plots in the whole area. Bald Ridge, at 7,000 feet (2134 m) altitude, is an 8-mile (12 km) long, gently undulating alpine area with numerous tarns and uninhibited views across to the spectacular peaks of the Selkirks. The hike is 14 miles to trail's end.

Begin as with the Beaver River trail. At Mile 4 (6 km), just before the main trail crosses Grizzly Creek, the trail forks. Follow the left fork up Grizzly Creek for less than a mile, crossing on a footbridge which spans the creek just past a warden patrol cabin. This cabin is not open to the public except for emergency use.

The trail climbs the hillside and turns into Copperstain Creek high up, then contours along the 6,000-foot (1829 m) level until it reaches the upper valley and headwaters. Another warden patrol cabin is situated along the trail at this point. From trail's end, Bald Ridge is easily accessible. For the most part the Copperstain Creek trail goes through dense timber, giving the best views at the top end.

Book List

Bandoni, R. J. and A. F. Szczawinski. *Guide to Common Mushrooms of British Columbia*. Victoria: B. C. Provincial Museum, Handbook no. 24, 1976.

Chambers, Alan D., study co-ordinator. "Purcell Range Study: Integrated Resource Management for British Columbia Purcell Mountains." Unpublished paper submitted to B. C. Environment and Land Use Committee, 1973.

Clark, Lewis J. *Lewis Clark's Field Guide to Wild Flowers of Forest and Woodland in the Pacific Northwest*. Sidney, B.C.: Gray's Publishing Ltd., 1974.

Coward, Garth and Paul Presidente. *Wilderness Survival*. Victoria: Information Division, B.C. Forest Service/Outdoor Recreation Branch, Dept. of Recreation and Travel Industry, Government of B.C., 1976.

Kay, Dave and D. A. MacDonald. *Come with Me to Yesterday*. Cranbrook: Rocky Mountain Printing, 1972.

Lees, J. A. and W. J. Clutterbuck. *B. C. 1887: A Ramble in British Columbia*. London, Eng.: Longmans, Green and Co., 1889.

Peterson, Roger Tory. *A Field Guide to Western Birds*. Boston: Houghton Mifflin Co., 1969.

Putnam, William Lowell. *A Climber's Guide to the Interior Ranges of British Columbia*. 5th ed. New York: The American Alpine Club, 1971.

Smyth, Fred J. *Tales of the Kootenays*. Vancouver: J. J. Douglas Ltd., 1977.

Szczawinski, A. F. and G. A. Hardy. *Guide to Common Edible Plants of British Columbia*. Victoria: B.C. Provincial Museum, Handbook no. 20, 1972.

Thorington, J. Monroe. *The Purcell Range of British Columbia*. New York: The American Alpine Club, 1946.

Underhill, Ted. *Wild Berries of the Pacific Northwest*. Saanichton, B.C.: Hancock House, 1974.

Wheeler, A. O. and Elizabeth Parker. *The Selkirk Mountains: A Guide for Mountain Climbers and Pilgrims*. Winnipeg: Stovel Company, 1912.